Intergenerational Income Mobility and Redistributive Policy

Mareike Schad

Intergenerational Income Mobility and Redistributive Policy

Springer Gabler

Mareike Schad
München, Germany

Technische Universität München, 2014

ISBN 978-3-658-10464-1 ISBN 978-3-658-10465-8 (eBook)
DOI 10.1007/978-3-658-10465-8

Library of Congress Control Number: 2015942506

Springer Gabler

Printed on acid-free paper

Springer Gabler is a brand of Springer Fachmedien Wiesbaden
Springer Fachmedien Wiesbaden is part of Springer Science+Business Media
(www.springer.com)

Acknowledgments

First and foremost I would like to thank Professor Robert K. von Weizsäcker. He has been an excellent supervisor and mentor, offering guiding advice and inspiring encouragement. I would also like to thank Professor Alwine Mohnen who agreed to serve as second supervisor on my thesis committee for her helpful comments. Additionally, Professor Bernd Süßmuth deserves my thanks for representing Professor Alwine Mohnen at my doctoral thesis defense. Furthermore, I am grateful to Professor Martin Moog, who completes my thesis committee as third examiner, for willingly accepting this office.

Furthermore, I would like to thank my colleagues from the *Lehrstuhl für Volkswirtschaftslehre* at the *Technische Universität München*, who provided me with a very pleasurable work and research environment. I am grateful for their advice that helped to advance my research project as well as for many fruitful lunch discussions.

I am indebted to my family and friends for supporting me while I was working on this thesis, especially Kathrin Schad and Johannes Berger for their understanding, support, and encouragement. Last, but by no means least, I am indebted to my parents Karl and Maria Schad for their love and support.

Mareike Schad

Abstract

Redistributive policy measures may reduce economic inequality and promote greater equality of opportunity. Whether such measures also increase intergenerational income mobility is the central issue in this thesis.

Focusing on education, the first part of this thesis analyzes the influence of education policy on intergenerational income mobility. It turns out that this influence crucially depends on how public and private human capital investments interdepend on each other. In addition, the impact of education on the strength of the economic parent-child connection is empirically investigated for Germany. The analysis includes factors such as education and occupation in order to explain intergenerational income immobility. Here education proves to be the most important mechanism through which economic advantages and disadvantages are passed across generations in Germany. Thus, according to both theory and empirical evidence, human capital accumulation is vital to economic success.

The second part of this thesis addresses social beliefs regarding the main determinants of economic success that emerge due to personal income mobility experiences. In fact, differences in social beliefs across countries may explain international differences in incentives to work and the preferences for the welfare state. The prevalent intergenerational income mobility within society is affected by inequality of opportunity as well as the individual's willingness to invest in effort. Policy measures that promote greater equality of opportunity may increase or decrease incentives to work. Therefore whether these policy measures additionally increase intergenerational income mobility is ambiguous. This depends on social beliefs as well as the degree of dynastic altruism within societies.

Contents

II Social Beliefs about Income Mobility and the Demand for Redistribution

List of Figures

List of Tables

General Introduction and Motivation

"The past tends to devour the future."

Thomas Piketty[1]

With his book "Capital in the Twenty-First Century", Thomas Piketty doubtlessly caught the spirit of the age. He addresses the dynamics which drive the accumulation and distribution of capital, using a collection of data over twenty countries which ranges as far back as the eighteenth century. His main finding is striking: a small group of people becomes richer and richer, while most of the remainder stay poor. Transmitting their own wealth to the offspring, a few family dynasties control a large part economic resources. Hence, family background and thus birth rather than individual performance determines social status and economic success. Most likely income level is strongly persistent across generations. Thus, like Piketty (2014) states: "The past tends to devour the future." With a strong parent-child connection, it is hard to imagine that there is equality of opportunity. Assuming high levels of income inequality within society, the poor are stigmatized. In this case, intergenerational income mobility is important because there is much to gain when climbing up the income ladder. Shedding light on intergenerational income mobility both theoretically and empirically is the main subject of this thesis. In contrast to Piketty (2014), the focus is particularly in labor income.

Analyzing the economic parent-child connection, intergenerational income mobility describes the likelihood of social advancement and descent across generations. Hereinafter, intergenerational income mobility is also referred to as income mobility or simply mobility. With regard to social flexibility, high income mobility across generations is desirable in many respects. This preserves social harmony: in mobile societies everyone can make it from rags to riches because of skills, abilities, and individual performance. This implies that family background is not that important, therefore these societies tend to offer quite equal opportunities. In these societies income is also regarded to be fairly distributed. In addition, mobility affects the efficacy and efficiency in society by

[1] Quoted in Piketty (2014, page 378).

setting additional incentives to work and enabling the members in society to apply their skills and talents in an advantageously way for society. Thus, such a society taps its full economic potential.

Over the last decades, the gap between rich and poor has anew been widening in most industrialized countries.[2] Thus, calls for social justice are growing ever louder. Policy measures that reduce economic inequality within society may additionally offer more equal opportunities. One example of such measures is public education. Reviewing redistributive policy measures, equality of opportunity serves as a criterion of how issues of social justice are resolved.[3] However, in addition to equality of opportunity, the prevalent intergenerational income mobility is important to evaluate a society's income distribution and its changes across time and generations. With regard to the increasing income inequality in the last decades, there is a strand of literature stating that this is accompanied by a decline in intergenerational income mobility.[4] The central issue of this thesis is whether redistributive policy measures that may offer more equal opportunities are also successful in enhancing intergenerational income mobility.

Part I of this thesis deals with education and its influence on intergenerational income (im)mobility. In the form of intergenerational transfer payment, public education reduces economic inequality that exists across generations *ex ante*. At first, it is theoretically analyzed whether education policies tending to promote greater equality of opportunity also enhance intergenerational income mobility. In addition to the direct effect of public education on the degree of intergenerational mobility, there is an indirect effect, as it impacts parents' decision of how much to invest in a child's human capital. Here, parents face the trade-off between their own consumption and higher future income levels of their child by investing in the child's human capital. Whether public education is successful to enhance intergenerational mobility decisively depends on how the parent's react to these policy measures. For example, if public education lowers the parent-child connection by crowding-out private human

[2]For this, see for example Atkinson and Piketty (2007) and Atkinson, Piketty, and Saez (2011).

[3]In this context equality of opportunity means equal life chances for all citizens concerning schooling, occupation, and other areas of personal advancement, as stated by Weizsäcker (1999).

[4]For this, see for example Solon (2004).

capital investment, family background will become less important and mobility will increase.

An individual's human capital decisively influences his or her prospects of success, regardless of whether it is formed by public or private investment. Capturing the importance of human capital accumulation, the degree to which pathway factors, such as education and occupation, can explain the intergenerational transmission of income inequality is empirically investigated for Germany.The prevalent immobility that is attributed to one of these factors consists of two parts. For the pathway factor education for example, this depends on (i) the strength of parental influence on educational attainment and (ii) the return on human capital investment. In line with international evidence, this empirical investigation reveals education and occupation to be chief contributors to the existing intergenerational immobility in Germany.

Part II of this thesis addresses the impact of social beliefs regarding the determinants of personal economic success on society. If there is uncertainty about the main determinants of success in society, individual beliefs regarding the relative weighting of these determinants are formed by personal experiences of intergenerational income mobility. In societies that put a high weight on self-determined rather than exogenously determined factors, its members tend to invest highly in effort to work, but are averse to redistribution on a large scale.

When offering more equal opportunities, a society's demand for redistribution decreases, as income seems to be more fairly distributed. However, the aggregate effect on individual effort is ambiguous, crucially depending on social beliefs. Both prevalent inequality of opportunity and incentives to work significantly affect intergenerational income mobility. Hence, policy measures that promote greater equality of opportunity do not always enhance income mobility. In societies that have a sufficiently strong belief in self-determination as opposed to exogenous determination, such measures decrease intergenerational mobility.

The central question, reflecting on the impact of policy measures on intergenerational mobility, links both parts of this thesis. The economic parent-child connection works through several channels. Not all redistributive policy measures necessarily increase intergenerational income mobility. Whether policy measures also increase mobility depends on their ability to reduce the influence of family background regarding individual achievement or individual decision.

The studies in both parts of the thesis have several assumptions in common, one of them being that of dynastic altruism. This describes the fact that parents are interested in both their own consumption and the expected level of consumption of their children.[5] This prompts parents to invest in their child's human capital (Part I) and crucially affects incentives to work and individual preferences for redistribution (Part II). For the latter, the magnitude of dynastic altruism is vital for the success of policy measures that offer more equal opportunities in order to increase intergenerational income mobility.

[5]Barro (1974) already considers the possibility of dynastic altruism in which present and future generations are connected by intergenerational transfers.

Part I

Intergenerational Income Mobility and Education

Chapter 1

Introduction

Opportunities for economic success are usually not equal across individuals in a society; in fact, they are characterized by inherited social structures. During feudalism in medieval Europe personal economic success, and thus the distribution of income and wealth in society, was determined by the property passed from father to (first-born) son. In contrast, today education is one of the most important factors for personal economic success. However, family background still plays a crucial role, as parental income influences children's opportunities through investment in their human capital. Therefore income levels are to some degree persistent across generations. Shedding light on this persistence on both theoretical and empirical grounds is the subject of this part of the thesis.

Redistributive policy to reduce economic inequality may enhance intergenerational income mobility. For example, education policy diminishes the economic inequality that exists across generations *ex ante* and in addition may increase mobility. Apart from influencing income mobility, redistributive policy also affects equality of opportunity, which means equal life chances for all citizens concerning schooling, occupation, and other areas of personal advancement.[1] An individual's prospects of success are (at least partially) dependent on his or her social origins. Poverty, for example, tends to be passed from generation to generation. Education policy, as an investment in the human capital of the children in society, can be understood as intergenerational transfer payments. Such policies diminish long-term intergenerational inequality and promote greater equality of opportunity. Hence, education policy can be rationalized not only by efficiency arguments (e.g. external effects, imperfect capital markets), but also to promote greater equality of opportunity, for example a distributional argument.

---

[1] For this, see Weizsäcker (1999).

Part I of this thesis initially aims to analyze the influence of redistributive policy, namely education policy, on intergenerational income mobility in society (Chapter 3). Subsequently, Chapter 4 empirically investigates the main channels through which economic advantage and disadvantage are passed across generations, focusing on Germany. Here the role of education in transmitting income inequality across generations is examined further.

Looking first at Chapter 3, public education affects not only equality of opportunity and income mobility, but also the parents' behavior when it comes to investing in their children's human capital. Investing in a child's human capital enhances his or her prospects of success. Therefore parents have to decide how much of their available income they are willing to spend as human capital investment in their child, facing the trade-off between their own consumption and a higher income for their children through such investment. When analyzing the effect of education policy on the degree of intergenerational mobility, besides the direct effect, its indirect effects on individual behavior—namely parent's reaction to varying education policies—is explicitly taken into account. The optimal level of private investment in the child's human capital increases with both parental income and the future earnings' rate of return of human capital investment.

In addition, the level of private investment in human capital depends on public education, allowing for the three potential interactive effects of public and private human capital investment: (i) public and private human capital investment are substitutes for each other, (ii) there is no relationship between public and private human capital investment, and (iii) public and private human capital investment are complements. It turns out that the underlying interactive effect of public and private human capital investment is vital for the success of education policy in enhancing intergenerational income mobility. Only if public education crowds out private human capital investment, the implementation of such education policy will increase intergenerational income mobility. Put differently, if public and private human capital investment complement each other, public education will decrease intergenerational income mobility. Hence, in addition to affecting parents' behavior, education policy significantly influences intergenerational income mobility. Beneficial for individual prospects of success, human capital substantially influences intergenerational income mobility.

Here family background and the return to education strongly determines an individual's level of human capital and thus his or her prospects of success.

Capturing the importance of human capital formation, the mechanisms that underlie income persistence across generations in Germany were empirically analyzed in Chapter 4. Here the focus is on the role of education in the intergenerational transmission process, but also other potential pathway factors are taken into account for transmitting economic advantage and disadvantage across generations, such as occupation and labor market attachment. In this context intergenerational income immobility—as a measure of the size of the economic parent-child connection—is decomposed into its direct and indirect components. Here the direct components are any factors not explained by the pathway factors included in this analysis. The indirect components measure the extent to which income persistence across generations is explained by the pathway factors. For example, examining education as a pathway of intergenerational transmission, the indirect component consists of (i) the effect of parental income on educational attainment and (ii) the influence of education on economic success. Thus, in line with theory, the indirect component comprises the influence of family background on educational attainment and the return to education. It turns out that at least one-fifth of the income persistence in Germany is explained solely by education. To insure robustness, the findings for Germany are compared to those for Great Britain and the United States as measured by Blanden, Haveman, Smeeding, and Wilson (2014). Education and occupation are the main channels in all three nations through which economic advantage and disadvantage are passed across generations. However, there are large differences in the explanatory power as well as the existing income mobility across the nations mainly because of varying returns on specific pathways.

Part I is organized as follows: Chapter 2 points out connections to the existing literature on this topic. Chapter 3 theoretically addresses the influence of public education on intergenerational income mobility within society. Chapter 4 empirically investigates mechanisms that underlie income persistence in Germany. Finally, Chapter 5 summarizes Part I.

Chapter 2

Related Literature

Economic mobility across generations is important in terms of equity and efficiency. Recently intergenerational income mobility has aroused great interest in the field of economics. With regard to empirical studies, this new interest can be explored through improved measurement methods and superior available data, which enables us to better quantify economic persistence across generations. This chapter reviews literature not only on income persistence across generations, but also on the link between intergenerational mobility and education. The review is divided into two parts: first the related theory-based literature is presented, and second the empirical studies on the issue of intergenerational mobility are reviewed, especially for the United States and Germany. This literature review focuses on the topic at hand; more extensive reviews on the topic of intergenerational economic mobility can be found in Björklund and Jäntti (2000); Blanden (2005, 2013); Corak (2006); Solon (2002).

Theory-Based Literature

The influence of governmental policies, especially education policy, on income mobility forms the basis of Weizsäcker (1999). In an exploratory model he investigates whether public education, in addition to promoting greater equality of opportunity, always results in a higher degree of mobility and less economic inequality. According to his research, even if society agrees on the aim of greater equality of opportunity, governmental policy is what decides whether more mobility is actually realized. The model distinguishes between policies pursuing integration and those pursuing differentiation. The aim of integration is realized by comprehensive schools ("Einheitsschulen"). In that type of school, the governmental investment effect is not linked to individuals. Accordingly, each individual in society benefits to the same extent from a specific level of education expenditures. The aim of differentiation is pursued in performance schools ("Leistungschulen"). In this case, the effect of public education expenditures depends on individual capabilities. As shown in

Weizsäcker (1999), in contrast to comprehensive schools, a rise in public education expenditures not always increase income mobility in society in the case of performance schools.

The study presented in Chapter 3 is related to Weizsäcker (1999), but the behavior of individuals within a society is explicitly taken into account and thus parents' trade-off between their own consumption and a higher income of their children through private investments in the child's human capital. In line with Weizsäcker (1999), the effect of *ex post* redistributive policy is also investigated. Here, intragenerational lump-sum transfer payments are considered, financed by income taxation. Families with below average incomes benefit from the implementation of redistributive taxation and thus inequality decreases. As a result, private investments assimilate more strongly across society and "self-made" inequality decreases. Confirming the findings in Weizsäcker (1999), redistributive taxation increases income mobility as more similar individual resources yield more equal opportunities for the children within the society.

The first to provide an economic model of intergenerational income mobility were Becker and Tomes (1986). In their paper (as well as in Becker and Tomes 1979), they consider the intergenerational transmission of inequality and the allocation of resources within a family. Becker and Tomes show that with perfect capital market, earnings are identified by endowments and thus inheritability. In that case, even if parents invest in the human capital of their child, parental income and human capital investment are not related. Therefore parent and child incomes are entirely linked through the inheritance of characteristics that are rewarded in the labor market.

With imperfect capital markets however, Becker and Tomes (1986) show that families with capital constraints (mostly referred to as "poor") cannot always invest optimally in their child's human capital. In that case, due to borrowing constraints, equality of opportunity and family wealth are thus related. Hence, as mobility can be enhanced either through the school system, which weakens the heritability of endowments, or by supporting higher education if credit constraints are binding, public policy has great power in encouraging mobility. Becker and Tomes (1986) address intergenerational transmission of economic inequality across generations, thereby assuming utility-maximizing parents who care about the welfare of their offspring. Starting with this initial contribution, further literature emerged based on the Becker-Tomes framework. For example, Checci, Ichino, and Rustichini (1999) extend the model of Becker and Tomes, examining the impact of education financing on intergenerational income mobility.

Building on the Becker-Tomes framework as well, Solon (2004) presents intergenerational income mobility as a function of parental investment and state investment in a child's human capital. According to his study, a country will display less intergenerational mobility than other countries if heritability is greater, human capital investment is more productive, return on human capital is higher, and/or public human capital investment is less progressive. Therefore education plays an important role in (not) generating intergenerational persistence. In addition, Solon shows that the link between parental income and a child's human capital, as well as the return on human capital, are crucial in transmitting economic status across generations. In his study Solon assumes that public investment in a child's human capital crowds out private parental investment. However, a crowding-out effect is not the only plausible interaction of public and private human capital investments.[1] In contrast to Solon, when investigating the influence of education policy on intergenerational income mobility in Chapter 3, different interactions between public and private human capital investments are taken into account which his model does not consider. Existing intergenerational income mobility within a society not only depends on public education policy, but also on its influence on private investment in a child's human capital. Hence, whether education policy measures increase intergenerational income mobility hinges on the interactive effect of public and private human capital investment.

Empirical Literature

Regarding empirical evidence on intergenerational economic mobility, there is recently a growing number of empirical studies which quantify income persistence across generations. On the one hand, for some industrialized countries superior data about individual (lifetime) income over various generations are

[1] Mayer and Lopoo (2008) for example, who investigate the link between government spending and intergenerational income mobility, only assume a crowding-out effect of private human capital investment through public education for high-income parents in the case of credit constraints.

available, as for the United States and Germany. On the other hand, the methods of measurement have improved and thus the bias of empirical estimates is narrowed.

Measurement error, unrepresentative samples, and life-cycle bias are the main methodological problems which especially early studies are faced with in estimating income persistence across generations.[2] In this regard, the studies of Solon (1992) and Zimmerman (1992) demonstrate a breakthrough in estimating intergenerational income immobility. Both conduct empirical studies which quantify the long-term correlation of income between generations in the United States. Solon quantifies the long-term correlation of incomes (more precisely, earnings) between generations in the United States of at least 0.4 based on data of the *Panel Study of Income Dynamics*. Zimmerman confirms the value of 0.4 for the United States by using data from the *National Longitudinal Survey* and taking into account different methods of measurement. Both studies are thus based on nationally representative samples[3] and alleviate measurement error by averaging fathers' earnings over four or five years of annual data. Since then a multitude of empirical studies have been conducted which quantify economic persistence across generations within a country.

After the contribution of Solon (1992) and Zimmerman (1992), early empirical studies quantify the average economic immobility across generations for specific countries. Generally when estimating economic immobility, the empirical literature uses income or earnings as a measure of the economic status of an individual. In addition, most of the empirical studies—and even all of the empirical studies which are mentioned here—determine either the intergenerational income (earning) elasticity or the income (earning) correlation across generations, thereby assuming a log-linear relationship of lifetime incomes (earnings).[4] The correlation measure allows for different levels of inequality between generations and thus changes in inequality across generations,

[2]For this and for a detailed discussion of methodological problems see, for example, Blanden (2009).

[3]In contrast to an earlier study of Behrman and Taubman (1985) in which there are measurement errors in fathers' earnings and unrepresentative samples. However, as one of the first, Behrman and Taubman estimate the intergenerational earnings immobility between fathers and sons, amounting to around 0.23.

[4]In the following, this log-linear relationship is assumed.

whereas the elasticity measure does not.[5] In later studies quantile regressions are also included, responding to the issue of whether the degree of mobility varies for different income brackets.

An example of recent evidence on intergenerational income mobility for the United States is the work of Mazumder (2005). He estimates the intergenerational earnings elasticity to be around 0.6 using administrative data containing the earning histories of parents and children. Hence, according to his study, the United States is even less mobile than previous research indicated. Compared to previous studies, as those of Solon (1992) and Zimmerman (1992), Mazumder uses longer-term data of father earnings.

For Germany several studies quantify the intergenerational economic mobility. Recently, Schnitzlein (2008) estimates that on average about 17 percent of a father's income advantage and disadvantage, respectively, are bequeathed to sons and about 20 percent are bequeathed to daughters. At the periphery of the distribution, however, substantially more persistence of economic advantage and disadvantage prevails.

The intergenerational earnings elasticity of around 0.2, as estimated in Schnitzlein (2008), indicates considerably less immobility than, for example, the previous study of Wiegand (1997) predicts. According to Wiegand, intergenerational immobility in Germany amounts to about 0.32.[6] Even though both studies are based on data from the *German Socio-Economic Panel*, rather large differences in the estimated intergenerational immobility occur. This fact highlights the sensitivity of findings concerning data collection and measurement method. For the two German studies different characteristics in the sample, as for example differences in the average age of the cohort, are likely responsible for the differences in the estimated earnings elasticity across generations. Thus estimation results of different studies should only be compared carefully. However, comparison of different studies, in particular across countries, is unavoidable, as the interpretation of the individual findings of those kinds of studies are limited in responding to whether a society is highly mobile or not. The absolute degree of mobility within a society is - seen in isolation - less conclusive. Consequentially, an increasing number of papers address in-

[5]The connection between these two measures is presented in detail in Chapter 4.
[6]The study of Wiegand (1997) is quoted after Blanden (2009).

ternational comparisons of intergenerational economic mobility by conducting estimates for different countries using comparable data and same measurement methods. Such international comparison enables us to grade different countries regarding the existing income mobility within those countries.

In this context, Couch and Dunn (1997) estimate and compare intergenerational mobility in the United States and Germany. According to their measure, the intergenerational earnings elasticity in Germany is about 0.11 and the comparable elasticity in the United States is around 0.13. In order to achieve comparability between Germany and the United States, Couch and Dunn use relatively young samples which at least in part explains the low estimates. Even though absolute findings may be biased, the international comparison suggests that earnings mobility across generations is nearly the same in both countries.

A more recent study of Vogel (2006), who also compares the intergenerational earnings mobility in the United States and Germany, points out that the United States is relatively more rigid than Germany. According to Vogel intergenerational earnings elasticity amounts to about 0.24 in Germany and about 0.34 in the United States. Since the late 2000s, some papers review and compare the empirical literature in the field of intergenerational economic mobility within and across countries. Examples of such literature reviews are Solon (2002) and Corak (2006).

Mobility across generations is also an important topic in sociology research. Here intergenerational mobility is measured in class or status rather than income. Taking this strand of literature into account, Björklund and Jäntti (2000) provide a literature review comparing the economic approach measuring intergenerational earning and income mobility with the two classical sociological approaches. In doing this they find out that in the United States mobility across generations seems to be relatively high in terms of class and status, but relatively low in terms of earning or income.

Related to Björklund and Jäntti (2000), Blanden (2013) summarizes the literature on intergenerational mobility, which are either classified by income, education or social class. In this she confirms that with regard to intergenerational mobility, in international comparison the United States is ranked differently for various measures: in terms of social class the United States appears to be relatively mobile, whereas in terms of income and education to be relatively immobile. In contrast, in Germany intergenerational mobility is relatively high in terms of income, but relatively low in terms of social class and education. In this context Germany and the United States form an exception, as for nearly all other countries considered in the study of Blanden the international rank is rather similar for the various measures of mobility. South America, the southern European nations and France seem to have rather limited mobility, while the opposite seems true for the Nordic countries. To explain the differences within and across countries, more should be known about what drives the persistence across generations.

Only recently the literature intensified its focus on the mechanisms that underlie economic persistence across generations. In this context Black and Devereux (2010), who provide one of the latest literature reviews on intergenerational mobility, emphasize that these developments are mostly attributed to the contribution of Solon (1999). While in the past only little attention was being paid to the processes that underlie earnings persistence, Solon addresses the intergenerational transmission of individual earnings status across generations.

In addition Bowles and Gintis (2002) investigate the process of intergenerational transmission of economic advantage and disadvantage. Here they decompose the intergenerational economic persistence in the direct effect of parental income and indirect effects operating through various channels, such as education. According to their estimation results, wealth, race, and schooling play important roles in the United States for the inheritance of economic status, but not the level of individual intelligence.

In line with these latest developments, in Chapter 4 the main forces are investigated that drive the relationship between parent and child incomes in Germany, in particular focusing on education as a possible channel through which economic advantage and disadvantage are passed across generations. In this context Blanden (2005) already analyzes the role of education in explaining the differences in mobility across the United Kingdom, the United States, West Germany and Canada. According to her, education has a great importance in explaining intergenerational transmission. Education is particularly crucial in driving the large immobility in the United States. The contribution of Blanden differs from my own contribution in Chapter 4 in many ways, starting with the approach. Applying the approach of Bowles and Gintis (2002) for Germany, in the empirical research presented in Chapter 4 several potential channels were investigated through which economic advantage and disadvantage are passed across generations including, for example, education and occupation.

Focusing on the role of education in driving intergenerational mobility, Hertz et al. (2007) show that in the United States education accounts for more than a third of the intergenerational income elasticity (with an estimated elasticity of around 0.53). For the United Kingdom, Blanden, Gregg, and Macmillan (2007) investigate the role of cognitive skills, non-cognitive traits, educational attainment and labor market attachment in explaining how parents with more income produce higher earning sons. According to them, these factors account for half of the association between parental income and children's earnings.

Recently, Blanden et al. (2014) examined the relationship underlying the estimated intergenerational elasticity in Great Britain and the United States. Applying the decomposition approach by Bowles and Gintis (2002), they analyzed the explanatory power of several factors, such as education, occupation, and labor market attachment, in transmitting income inequality across generations. Substantial differences were shown between the two countries; in the United States education is most important for the intergenerational transmission of income inequality, whereas in Great Britain occupation is primarily responsible for it. In Chapter 4, the explanatory power of those pathway factors are empirically estimated in the case of Germany. Following the same approach and including the same potential pathways of intergenerational transmission as Blanden et al. makes international comparison possible which is important for robustness of the results.

Chapter 3

Education Policy and Intergenerational Income Mobility

Public investment in human capital may be beneficial for two reasons: on the one hand they promote equal opportunity, on the other hand they may have a redistributive effect. In addition, besides private human capital investment, education policy may affect intergenerational income mobility.

This chapter addresses the issue of whether and how education policy influences the degree of intergenerational income mobility within a society. Initially, the main assumptions and findings of Weizsäcker (1999), including the effect of two different education policy measures on the intergenerational income correlation, are briefly summarized in Section 3.1. In Section 3.2 the effect of education policy on mobility is analyzed for varying education policy measures. Here the effects of both public education and private human capital investment on mobility is explicitly investigated. Hence, the individual's response to public education is determined, taking into account the various interactions of public and private human capital investment. The impact of public and private human capital investments on intergenerational income mobility is then analyzed for the different kinds of interactions. Finally, in Section 3.3 the results are discussed and compared.

3.1 Public Education and Equality of Opportunity

A brief summary of Weizsäcker (1999) is done in this section enabling us to compare his results with the findings achieved in the subsequent sections. Weizsäcker first addresses the influence of income taxation on intergenerational mobility. Secondly, he investigates the impact of public education on economic mobility and income distribution within a society.

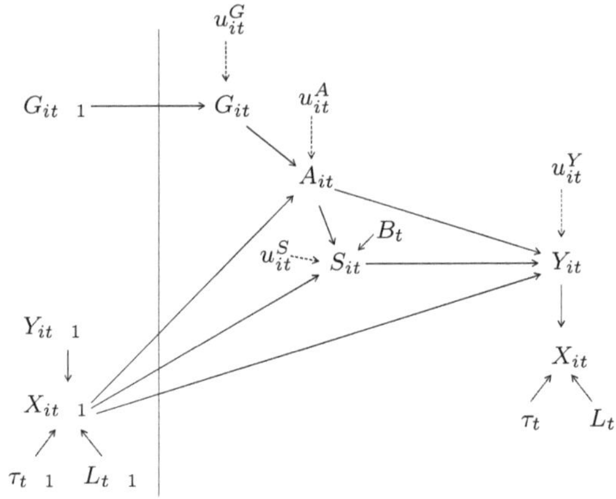

Figure 3.1: Intergenerational Relations Presented in Weizsäcker (1999)

3.1.1 Intergenerational Correlation of Lifetime Incomes

Weizsäcker (1999) determines the intergenerational correlation of lifetime income on the basis of the intergenerational relations presented in Figure 3.1. Those relationships demonstrate empirically the best-supported interactions of the most important determinants of economic success. Herein G is the genetic basic endowment; A stands for abilities (e.g., the measured IQ); S denotes education (e.g., qualification); and Y describes economic success, which can be interpreted as gross lifetime income. In the basic version of the model the governmental role is restricted to pure redistributive taxation. The tax rate is stated by τ and the governmental lump-sum transfer payment by L. The available income is denoted by X and the stochastic noise by u. In addition to luck, u also comprises all determinants which are not explicitly modeled. The index t identifies the generation considered and i marks a representative dynasty. Assuming that the government invests in education of the children within society, B stands for public education expenditure per capita.

According to the theoretical and empirical insights, economic success of an individual mainly depends on family background, his or her abilities, and his or her qualifications. The direct effects on economic success are thus described by y_A, y_S, and y_X, whereas index A, for example, stands for the direct effect of abilities on individual economic success. Abilities A_{it} are determined by the family background X_{it-1} and the hereditary factor G_{it}. The individual hereditary factor is a function of the parental hereditary factor G_{it-1} and is given by:

$$G_{it} = gG_{it-1} + u_{it}^G. \tag{3.1}$$

With the empirically supported assumption $0 < g < 1$, Equation (3.1) displays the typical characteristic of a regression against the mean. Finally, in the absence of public education, the achieved qualification level S_{it} depends on individual abilities A_{it} and family background X_{it-1}. The indirect effects of economic success (via abilities and the achieved qualification levels, respectively) are illustrated by a_G, a_X, s_A, and s_X.

The available income of individual i of generation t is consistent with after-tax income plus the governmental transfer payments:

$$X_{it} = (1-\tau)Y_{it} + L_t \tag{3.2}$$
$$\text{with} \quad 0 \leq \tau \leq 1 \quad \text{and} \quad L_t > 0.$$

In the basic version of the model abstracting from public education, the government is restricted to pure redistributive taxation. The governmental budget constraint is:

$$L_t = \tau \cdot \mu_{Y_t}, \tag{3.3}$$

with μ_{Y_t} the average lifetime income in generation t. From the formalization of the intergenerational relations presented in Figure 3.1, the following formal connection arises:

$$Y_{it} = \alpha G_{it} + \beta X_{it-1} + \epsilon_{it} \tag{3.4}$$

with:

$$\alpha = a_G(y_A + s_A y_S),$$
$$\beta = a_X(y_A + s_A y_S) + s_X y_S + y_X, \quad 0 < \beta < 1,$$
$$\epsilon_{it} = (y_A + s_A y_S)u_{it}^A + y_S u_{it}^S + u_{it}^Y.$$

The direct and indirect effects on economic success are combined based on the initial relations. Parameter β indicates the influence of family background on economic success. β together with the parameter g constitutes the central intergenerational linking parameters. α is a weighing parameter which describes how strongly economic success depends on hereditary factors. The random variable u_{it}^G and the residual ϵ_{it}, respectively, are assumed to be stochastic independent over all i and t, as well as from the particular state variable. It is assumed that the society is sufficiently large such that random sample moments approximately agree with the theoretical moments. In the long run, the variance of the available lifetime income within a generation is given as follows:

$$\sigma_X^2 = \frac{(1-\tau)^2}{1-(1-\tau)^2\beta^2}\left[\alpha^2\sigma_G^2\frac{1+(1-\tau)\beta g}{1-(1-\tau)\beta g} + \sigma_\epsilon^2\right]. \tag{3.5}$$

In the model the immobility of the available lifetime income between generations is determined by the coefficient of autocorrelation. Hence, without public education the immobility equates[1]:

$$\rho_{XX_{-1}} = \frac{Cov(X, X_{-1})}{\sigma_X^2} = (1-\tau)\beta + \frac{\left[1-(1-\tau)^2\beta^2\right]g}{1+(1-\tau)\beta g + \frac{1-(1-\tau)\beta g}{\alpha^2}\frac{\sigma_\epsilon^2}{\sigma_G^2}}. \tag{3.6}$$

The coefficient of autocorrelation $\rho_{XX_{-1}}$, a standard measure in both the theoretical and empirical literature, quantifies the existing intergenerational link between generations: the lower the coefficient of autocorrelation, the higher the intergenerational income mobility in society. Together with the long-term tax rate:

$$\tau = \frac{L}{\mu_Y} = \frac{(1-\beta)L}{\alpha\mu_G + \mu_\epsilon} = \tau(\overset{-}{\alpha}, \overset{-}{\beta}, \overset{-}{\mu_G}, \overset{-}{\mu_\epsilon}, \overset{+}{L}),$$

[1]Due to long-term consideration, the variance of income is assumed to be the same across generations.

Equation (3.6) generates the basis for further comparative investigations. The findings of the connections between the intergenerational linking parameters and $\rho_{XX_{-1}}$ is as follows:

$$\frac{d\rho_{XX_{-1}}}{d\beta} > 0 \quad \text{and} \quad \frac{d\rho_{XX_{-1}}}{d\alpha} > 0.$$

Both α and β positively affect the coefficient of autocorrelation. Hence, a reduction in either α or β increases intergenerational income mobility in society. Reducing β means that the long-term correlation of the economic status of parents and children decreases and thus income mobility rises. Public policies that diminish the advantage of being born in a wealthy family and the disadvantage of coming from a poor family reduce β and bring about greater equality of opportunity. Hence, public measures that reduce β promote equality of opportunity and simultaneously increase social mobility. The claim of greater equality of opportunity, however, also includes public policies that abolish barriers to talented individuals. Such policy measures result in a rise in α which in turn entails a reduction in mobility. Accordingly, such public measures promote greater equality of opportunity by raising α and thus lowering intergenerational income mobility. Consequently, whether promoting greater equality of opportunity increases income mobility depends on the public policy measure applied.

A reduction of the stochastic noise, appearing in a lower variance of ϵ, strengthens the parent-child correlation and thus decreases intergenerational income mobility in society. The resulting effect of variations in σ_ϵ^2 disclose the importance of distinguishing between inequality and mobility. Reducing σ_ϵ^2 decreases intergenerational mobility and simultaneously reduces the variance of available lifetime income. While the effect on available lifetime income is desirable, the effect on mobility is not. Public measures in educational policy often simultaneously affect α, β and σ_ϵ^2, and thus the parent-child connection through different channels. As a consequence the net effect on intergenerational income mobility in society is *ex ante* unknown.

Finally, the comparison of the intergenerational correlation $\rho_{XX_{-1}}$ of the available lifetime income with the resulting intergenerational correlation $\rho_{YY_{-1}}$

of the gross lifetime income yields:

$$\rho_{YY_{-1}}|_{\tau=L=0} > \rho_{XX_{-1}}.$$

Consequently, the implementation of redistributive taxation raises intergenerational income mobility within society.

3.1.2 Impact of Public Education Policy

The second part of Weizsäcker (1999) addresses the influence of public education on mobility. More precisely, he investigates whether intergenerational income mobility increases if education expenditures per capita increases, assuming different types of schools. Here, it is assumed that education expenditure affects the level of education by the resultant school quality:

$$Q_t = f(B_t) \quad \text{with} \quad f^{'} > 0 > f^{''}.$$

A rise of per capita education expenditure increases the quality of education. However, additional quality resulting from a marginal increase of per capita education expenditure decreases with the amount already invested. The level of public education expenditure as well as the level of redistribution are exogenously given.[2]

First, comprehensive schools ("Einheitsschulen") are considered where the aim of integration is pursued. In this case, the public investment effect is not linked with the individual. Accordingly, all individuals benefit to the same extent from a given increase of per capita education expenditure B_t. In case of comprehensive schools, the achieved individual qualification level is formalized as follows:

$$S_{it} = s_A A_{it} + s_X X_{it-1} + s_B Q_t + u_{it}^S \tag{3.7}$$

and thus, personal economic success of an individual is determined as follows:

$$Y_{it} = \alpha G_{it} + \beta X_{it-1} + \gamma Q_t + \epsilon_{it} \tag{3.8}$$

[2]In the case of public education policy, the governmental budget constraint is given by $\tau \mu_{Y_t} = L_t + B_{t+1}$.

with:

$$\begin{aligned}
\alpha &= a_G(y_A + s_A y_S),\\
\beta &= a_X(y_A + s_A y_S) + s_X y_S + y_X, \quad 0 < \beta < 1,\\
\gamma &= s_B y_S\\
\epsilon_{it} &= (y_A + s_A y_S)u_{it}^A + y_S u_{it}^S + u_{it}^Y.
\end{aligned}$$

Taking into account the long-term tax rate[3] and the resultant coefficient of autocorrelation:

$$\rho_{XX_{-1}} = \rho_{XX_{-1}}(\overset{+}{\alpha}, \overset{+}{\beta}, \overset{-}{\sigma_\epsilon^2}; \overset{-}{\tau}\ (\overset{-}{\alpha}, \overset{+}{\beta}, \overset{-}{L}, \overset{-}{\gamma}, \overset{+}{Q}\ (\overset{+}{B}), \overset{+}{B})) \tag{3.9}$$

Weizsäcker highlights the relation between immobility across generations and per capita education expenditure as follows:

$$\frac{d\rho_{XX_{-1}}}{dB} < 0 \quad (\text{with} \quad \frac{d\tau}{dB} > 0).$$

The impact of public education expenditure on income mobility is determined by the effect of public education expenditure on the tax rate τ and its retroactive effect on ρ. In the case of comprehensive schools, higher education expenditure always increases intergenerational income mobility.

Second, the impact of increased education expenditures on income mobility across generations is analyzed in the case of performance schools ("Leistungsschulen"). This type of school pursues the aim of differentiation and hence the public investment effect hinges on individual training potential. Assuming that a percentage increase of B yields the same percentage increase of the level of education for all i, the achieved individual qualification level is formally given by the following multiplied combination:

$$S_{it} = (s_A A_{it} + s_X X_{it-1} + u_{it}^S) \cdot Q_t(B). \tag{3.10}$$

[3]The long-term tax rate is $\tau = \frac{L+B}{\mu_Y} = \frac{(1\ \ \beta)(L+B)}{\alpha\mu_G+\mu_\epsilon+\gamma Q(B)\ \ \beta B}$, resulting from the governmental budget constraint.

Accordingly, personal economic success arises as follows:

$$Y_{it} = \alpha(B) \cdot G_{it} + \beta(B) \cdot X_{it-1} + \epsilon_{it}(B) \tag{3.11}$$

with:

$$\begin{aligned}
\alpha &= a_G(y_A + s_A y_S Q) = \alpha(B), \\
\beta &= a_X(y_A + s_A y_S Q) + s_X y_S Q + y_X = \beta(B), \quad 0 < \beta < 1, \\
c_{it} &- (y_A + s_A y_S Q)u_{it}^A + y_S Q u_{it}^S + u_{it}^Y = \epsilon_{it}(B).
\end{aligned}$$

Individuals with high training potential benefit more from a certain quality of education $Q(B)$ than individuals with lower training potential. In that case the impact of education expenditure on the correlation of the available lifetime income is given by:

$$\rho_{XX_{-1}} = \rho_{XX_{-1}}(\overset{+}{\alpha}\,(\overset{+}{B}), \overset{+}{\beta}\,(\overset{+}{B}), \overset{-}{\sigma_\epsilon^2}\,(\overset{+}{B}); \overset{-}{\tau}\,(\overset{-}{\alpha}\,(\overset{+}{B}), \beta(\overset{+}{B}), \overset{+}{L}, \overset{+}{B})). \tag{3.12}$$

Personal economic success is only indirectly affected by education expenditure: the effect of state education investment on income mobility is covered by the tax effect via τ as well as by the linking parameters α and β and the stochastic variable ϵ. The overall effect (and thus the sign of $d\rho_{XX_{-1}}/dB$) is not unambiguously determinable. Hence, a rise in state education expenditures does not always increase intergenerational income mobility. Even if unanimity exists about the fundamental aim of promoting equal opportunity, it depends on the public measure as to whether it also results in more economic mobility.

3.2 Public Education and Private Human Capital Investment

Dependent on the objectives pursued, education policy may increase intergenerational economic mobility. Here, whether economic mobility increases hinges on the underlying interaction of public and private human capital investments.

Parents face the trade-off between their own consumption and a higher income of their children through private investment in their human capital. Public education affects parental decision about the level of investment in their children's human capital. Hence, the effect of public education on intergenerational mobility consists of a direct effect and its indirect effects on individual behavior.

The aim of this section is to analyze the effects of public education on intergenerational income mobility taking into account various interactions of public and private human capital investments, as for example a complementary relation. Before investigating the influence of education policies on mobility, individual behavior concerning private human capital investment is determined in absence of public education.

3.2.1 Private Human Capital Investment and Income Mobility

An overlapping generation model is considered in which two generations live at the same time, namely the parent generation and the child generation. Each generation lives for two periods: in the first period, generation t is in its childhood. There, each individual receives public human capital investment B_{it} as well as private human capital investment I_{it}. In the second period, generation t is adult and realizes income Y_{it}, which in part is spent for consumption C_{it}. Here index i stands for a family dynasty and t marks the affiliation to a generation. For simplicity it is assumed that each individual has exactly one offspring: each family dynasty i consists of a parent of generation $t-1$ and a child of generation t.

Parents have the opportunity to enhance the prospects of success of their child by investment in the child's human capital. They are interested in prospects of success of their child as high as possible, as they benefit from the economic status of the child. The fact that parents are not only interested in their own consumption, but also in the potential economic status of their child is referred to as dynastic altruism.[4] Hence, parents have to decide how much of their available income they should invest in the child's education and how much they should spend on their own consumption. Consequentially, the parent of dynasty i in generation $t-1$ spends the amount C_{it-1} of his available

[4] Assuming that parents take the child's economic status instead of the child's consumption level into account is justified by the fact that the latter contains more uncertainty: at the time of decision parents do not know the consumption decision of the offspring generation.

income X_{it-1} for his own consumption and invests I_{it} in the child's human capital, where C_{it-1} and I_{it} take place simultaneously. Assuming that parents cannot borrow money at the cost of the prospective income of their children, the budget constraint a parent is faced with is given by:

$$X_{it-1} = C_{it-1} + I_{it}. \tag{3.13}$$

In the model governmental activity is financed by (proportional) income taxation. Hence, the available income X_{it-1} of dynasty i in generation $t-1$ depends on gross income Y_{it-1} as follows:

$$X_{it-1} = (1 - \tau)Y_{it-1}, \tag{3.14}$$

where τ indicates the income tax rate.

Human capital received in childhood positively affects economic success in adulthood. The received human capital consists of (private) parental human capital investment I_{it} and public human capital investment B_{it}, but for now the case of public education is excluded (that is $B_{it} = 0$). In addition to the amount of human capital investment received in childhood, the individual genetic basic endowment determines income Y_{it} in adulthood. Assuming that income is derived from the following semi-logarithmic earning function:[5]

$$\log Y_{it} = \omega \cdot H(I_{it}, B_{it}) + \varphi G_{it}, \tag{3.15}$$

the first term of the equation reflects the return of received human capital investment comprising I_{it} and B_{it}. The technology $H(I_{it}, B_{it})$ describes the transformation of human capital investment in human capital. The parameter ω specifies the earnings rate of return on human capital. Given different levels of private human capital investment, ω marks the extent of income inequality in society. The higher ω, the less equally distributed incomes are. Income is scaled logarithmically compressing Equation (3.15) along the dependent variable. This is justified by the fact that within a society income covers a large range, while the value range of human capital is relatively more restricted. The functional form implies that assuming $\omega = 0.1$ for example, a one unit increase

[5]Hereinafter the log function is understood as the natural logarithm.

in human capital would generate a ten percent increase in income. The second term of Equation (3.15) describes the effect of genetic basic endowment. In line with Weizsäcker (1999), the basic endowment depends on parental endowment according to Equation (3.1):

$$G_{it} = gG_{it-1} + u_{it}^{G}.$$

Hence, genetic basic endowment is independent of the level of human capital investment received. Interpretable in various ways, a detailed discussion of individual endowment G_{it} is provided in Becker and Tomes (1979). Put briefly, genetic basic endowment can, for example, be construed as (partially) inherited abilities of the child or as the amount of relations a child receives from his or her parents to increase earnings prospects. The characteristic of the individual endowment can be naturally given as well as resulting from nurture.

Without public education, the transformation of human capital investment in human capital is quantified by the following function:

$$H(I_{it}) = \phi \log I_{it}. \tag{3.16}$$

The level of human capital a child receives depends on private human capital investments I_{it} from parents. The parameter ϕ quantifies the productivity of human capital investment (with $\phi > 0$). Distinct from Equation (3.15), the function is compressed along the independent variable I_{it}, as the value range of H_{it} covers a relatively restricted range compared to the value range of I_{it}. Accordingly, a one hundred percent increase of private investments in human capital would cause a ϕ unit increase in human capital. Moreover, the marginal productivity of human capital decreases with the level of private human capital investment. In regards to completeness, in the model it is assumed that work effort is unified and normalized.

Optimal Level of Private Human Capital Investment

Parents of generation $t-1$ are interested in the best possible prospects of success of their child. They are faced with the decision of how much of their available income they spend for consumption and how much they should invest in the education of their child. As parents have no information about the level of consumption in the next generation,[6] they take into account the achievable economic status of their child. Hence, parent's utility depends on C_{it-1} and Y_{it} with the following functional form:

$$U_{it-1} = \log C_{it-1} + \gamma \log Y_{it}. \tag{3.17}$$

The parameter $\gamma \in (0,1)$ reflects the extent of dynastic altruism. The Cobb-Douglas utility function features the typical characteristics of positive, but decreasing, marginal utility in both C_{it-1} and Y_{it}. Hence, the marginal utility of an additional unit of consumption decreases with the level of C_{it-1} (analog for Y_{it}).

With due regard to the parental budget constraint (Equation (3.13)) and Equations (3.14), (3.15), and (3.16), the following maximization problem results from (3.17):

$$\max_{I_{it}} U_{it-1} = \log((1-\tau)Y_{it-1} - I_{it}) + \gamma(\omega\phi \log I_{it} + \varphi G_{it}). \tag{3.18}$$

The first order condition[7] yields the optimal level of private human capital investment:

$$I_{it} = \frac{\gamma\omega\phi}{1+\gamma\omega\phi}(1-\tau)Y_{it-1}. \tag{3.19}$$

The optimal level of private human capital investment *ceteris paribus* increases with parental income. The higher the parental income, the more they invest in the child's education. If investment in human capital pays off more, parents will be more willing to invest in their child's human capital. If productivity of human capital investment and earnings return on human capital are high (that is high ω and ϕ), investment in human capital will be more profitable. A growing degree of dynastic altruism (increasing γ) enhances the relative importance of the expected income status of the child Y_{it} and hence parents are *ceteris paribus* more willing to invest in the human capital of the child.

[6]Here the possibility that parents devolve their own decision between consumption and private investment to the decision taken by the next generation is excluded.

[7]The second order condition is fulfilled so that the resultant level of private human capital investment maximizes individual utility.

Intergenerational Income Elasticity

Assuming no governmental activity (that is $\tau = 0$) and incorporating the optimal level of private human capital investment, the parent-child connection is as follows:

$$\log Y_{it} = y^* + \omega\phi \log(Y_{it-1}) + \varphi G_{it} \tag{3.20}$$
$$\text{with} \quad y^* = \omega\phi \log(\frac{\gamma\omega\phi}{1+\gamma\omega\phi}).$$

If the state neither invests in education nor redistributes income *ex post*, available income will be equivalent to gross income. In addition to the particular conditions of an economy[8], personal economic success depends on individual hereditary factors and parental income. The first term of Equation (3.20) can be interpreted as basic income which depends on the general societal conditions—and thus, on the parameters ω, ϕ and γ. At first glance, Equation (3.20) seems like the log-linear intergenerational income regression applied in empirical studies measuring intergenerational income elasticity. The genetic basic endowment G_{it} as well as parental log income depends on genetic basic endowment of the parent (G_{it-1}). The (error) term φG_{it} is thus correlated with $\log Y_{it-1}$. Therefore Equation (3.20) represents a first-order autoregression of $\log Y_{it}$. φG_{it} itself is consistent with a first-order autoregression (Equation (3.1)). Taking into account these correlations, in the long run the steady-state intergenerational income elasticity is determined by the sum of the coefficients of Equations (3.20) and (3.1), divided by 1 plus its product.[9] Long-term consideration implies that $\log Y_{it-1}$ and $\log Y_{it}$ exhibit the same variance. In the absence of governmental measures, the long-term intergenerational income elasticity is thus:

$$\eta_{na} = \frac{\omega\phi + g}{1 + \omega\phi g}. \tag{3.21}$$

The index na marks the case of government absence. The intergenerational income elasticity η indicates the percentage increase of individual income if parental income rises by one percent. Hence measuring immobility between

[8] The economic condition comprises magnitudes of the variables ω, ϕ, and γ.

[9] The steady-state intergenerational income elasticity is in detail derived in Appendix A.1 and generally shown, for example, in Greene, 2000.

generations, income elasticity describes to what extent advantages and disadvantages of particular income classes are passed on to the next generation. In the model, hereditary factors comprise genetic basic endowment. A high level of G_{it} implies high individual income, whereas φ specifies the strength of this effect. If a child's genetic basic endowment heavily depends on the parents' genetic basic endowment, his or her income will be strongly correlated with parental income. Accordingly, the higher the heritability coefficient, the greater the long-term income elasticity. The earnings return of human capital investment $\omega\phi$ specifies to what extent investments in human capital are worthwhile for the achievable income of a child. The level of private human capital investment in a child increases with parental income and with the earnings return of human capital investment $\omega\phi$. The higher $\omega\phi$ is, the less equal both private investment in the children's human capital and the resultant income distribution within society are. The long-term intergenerational income elasticity is greater the more productive human capital investment is, and the higher the rate of return of human capital investment is.

Quantifying intergenerational income elasticity as a measure of immobility across generations does not allow for changes in income inequality between generations and thus across time, whereas the correlation measure does.[10] But in the long run, implying the same income inequality between generations, both measures yield the same intergenerational income immobility. Hence, when interpreting income in the model of Weizsäcker (1999) as log income, immobility measures are the same in both models.[11] The immobility in society increases with the earnings return of human capital and human capital investment, respectively, according to:

$$\frac{\partial \eta_{na}}{\partial \omega} > 0 \quad \text{and} \quad \frac{\partial \eta_{na}}{\partial \omega\phi} > 0.$$

This is in line with the results of Section 3.1.

[10]In Chapter 4, both measures are explained and compared in detail.

[11]Weizsäcker also assumes income inequality to be the same across generations. In contrast to Weizsäcker (1999), individual income is not determined stochastically, but is precisely defined dependent on genetic basic endowment and received human capital investment.

Redistributive Measures

Still abstracting from public education, it is assumed that the government redistributes income *ex post* by lump-sum transfer payments (denoted by L_{t-1}). As the lump-sum transfer has to be solely financed by the income tax, the governmental budget constraint is given by:

$$\tau \cdot \mu_{t-1} = L_{t-1},$$

where μ_{t-1} is the average income of generation $t-1$. The available parental income X_{it-1} depends on individual gross income Y_{it-1} and the governmental lump-sum transfer payments L_{t-1} as follows:

$$X_{it-1} = (1-\tau)Y_{it-1} + L_{t-1}. \tag{3.22}$$

When redistributing income, private human capital investments are then:[12]

$$I_{it} = \frac{\gamma\omega\phi}{1+\gamma\omega\phi}((1-\tau)Y_{it-1} + L_{t-1})$$

and income correlation is as follows:

$$\log Y_{it} = y^* + \omega\phi \log(\underbrace{(1-\tau)Y_{it-1} + L_{t-1})}_{X_{it-1}}) + \varphi G_{it}$$

$$\text{with} \quad y^* = \omega\phi \log(\frac{\gamma\omega\phi}{1+\gamma\omega\phi}).$$

When available parental income X_{it-1} and economic status of the child Y_{it} are taken into account, redistributing income does not alter intergenerational income elasticity. Income immobility across generations is still:

$$\eta_{na} = \frac{\omega\phi + g}{1+\omega\phi g}.$$

However, redistributive policy increases equality of opportunity, as the differences in private human capital investment dependent on parental income decrease. The consequences of an increase of the tax rate in society *ceteris*

[12] Taking into account the parental budget constraint (Equation (3.22)) and Equations (3.14), (3.15) and (3.16).

parisbus depends on the relative position in the social income distribution: families with below average incomes benefit from redistributive taxation. Thus, their level of private human capital investment increases with the tax rate. In contrast, in families with above average incomes, private investment in human capital decreases with an increasing tax rate, as they suffer losses from redistributive taxation.

3.2.2 Public Education, Private Human Capital Investment and Income Mobility

In this section, (i) the effect of public education on private human capital investment and (ii) the influence of both public and private human capital investments on intergenerational income mobility in society are analyzed. Here, the three possible interactions of public and private human capital investments are taken into account. In the following the role of the government is limited to education policy. Hence, tax revenues are solely used to provide public education. Public investment in human capital illustrates intergenerational transfer payments: taxpayers of generation $t-1$ pay for the education of generation t.

Crowding-Out of Public and Private Human Capital Investments

Most generally, in the literature a crowding-out effect of public and private human capital investments is assumed, as in Solon (2004). Assuming a crowding-out of private human capital investment through public education, the transformation of private and public human capital investment in a child's human capital can formally be expressed by:

$$H(I_{it}, B_{it}) = \phi \cdot \log(I_{it} + B_{it}), \tag{3.23}$$

dependent on private human capital investment I_{it}, public investment in human capital B_{it}, and the productivity of those investments ϕ. The marginal product of private human capital investment depends on the aggregate level of human capital investment in a child (that is, the sum of public and private human capital investments).

Considering the parental budget constraint (3.13) and the transformation of human capital investment in income (Equations (3.15) and (3.23)), the parental maximization problem, based on the individual utility function (3.17), results as:

$$\max_{I_{it}} U_{it-1} = \log((1-\tau)Y_{it-1} - I_{it}) + \gamma(\omega\phi\log(I_{it} + B_{it}) + \varphi G_{it}). \quad (3.24)$$

Thus, the optimal level of private human capital investment is given by:

$$I_{it} = \frac{\gamma\omega\phi}{1+\gamma\omega\phi}(1-\tau)Y_{it-1} - \frac{1}{1+\gamma\omega\phi}B_{it}. \quad (3.25)$$

Public and private investments in human capital are substitutes, as public education crowds out private investment in a child's human capital. Well-known examples for such public and private human capital investment are public and private schools, respectively. As school choice is an either-or decision, the example does not fit very well. Another example is private tutoring for a child, which is either publicly provided or financed by parents. If an increasing amount of private lessons is publicly provided, parents will invest less in private lessons for their child. The effects of γ, ω and ϕ on the parent's investment decision are the same as without public education: private investment in the child's human capital increases with parental income, with greater dynastic altruism, with more productive human capital investment, and with higher earnings return on human capital. Interpreting the productivity level ϕ as individual talent, private human capital investment would increase with a child's talent, as the realized human capital per unit of education investment increases. Consequently, if one were to consider heterogeneity of individual talent, more talented children *ceteris parisbus* would receive more private human capital investment.

In the model, tax revenues of the (proportional) income taxation are used to provide public education. Similar to Solon (2004), a society's education policy can formally be described as follows:

$$\frac{B_{it}}{(1-\tau)Y_{it-1}} \cong N - \nu\log Y_{it-1}, \quad (3.26)$$

whereas ν (with $0 < \nu < 1$) characterizes a kind of relative progressivity of public education expenditures. The absolute level of public education of children born into high-income families can be higher or lower than for children born into low-income families. However, the correlation of public investment to the parental after-tax income decreases with parental income. The higher

ν, the more progressive is the state education policy. The specific functional form of education policy implies the plausible assumption of progressivity of state education policy.

Taking into account the optimal level of private human capital investment, individual income in generation t results from Equation (3.15)—by plugging in (3.23) and (3.25)—as follows:

$$\log Y_{it} = \omega\phi \log(\frac{\gamma\omega\phi}{1+\gamma\omega\phi}) + \omega\phi \log((1-\tau)Y_{it-1} + B_{it}) + \varphi G_{it}. \tag{3.27}$$

For a sufficiently small relation $\frac{B_{it}}{(1-\tau)Y_{it-1}}$, the correlation of incomes between generations becomes:

$$\log Y_{it} \cong y_{co} + \omega\phi(1-\nu)\log Y_{it-1} + \varphi G_{it} \tag{3.28}$$
$$\text{with} \quad y_{co} = \omega\phi(N + \log(\frac{\gamma\omega\phi}{1+\gamma\omega\phi} \cdot (1-\tau)).$$

The derivation of this equation is in Appendix A.2.

Analog to the scenario of government absence, the long-term intergenerational income elasticity results from the slope coefficient of Equation (3.28) and the coefficient of autocorrelation of Equation (3.1) as follows:

$$\eta_{co} = \frac{\omega\phi(1-\nu)+g}{1+\omega\phi(1-\nu)g}. \tag{3.29}$$

The index *co* marks the case of crowding-out of private through public human capital investment. The long-term intergenerational income elasticity is greater, the higher the heritability coefficient g, the more productive human capital investment (ϕ) and the higher the earnings return on human capital ω is. As already mentioned, the correlation of state education investment to parental after-tax income decreases with increasing parental income. This effect gets weaker as ν becomes smaller. Accordingly, the less progressive state education investment is (lower ν), the higher the long-term intergenerational income elasticity.

No Effect of Public Education on Private Human Capital Investment

If the transformation of human capital investment in human capital is assumed to be:

$$H(I_{it}, B_{it}) = \phi \cdot (\log I_{it} + \log B_{it}), \tag{3.30}$$

the marginal product of private (public) human capital investment will be independent of the level of public (private) human capital investment.

Analog to the case of a crowding-out effect of public and private human capital investments, the maximization problem results from plugging in the Equations (3.13), (3.14), (3.15), and (3.30) in (3.17) and is thus given by:

$$\max_{I_{it}} U_{it-1} = \log((1-\tau)Y_{it-1} - I_{it}) + \gamma(\omega\phi \log(I_{it} \cdot B_{it}) + \varphi G_{it}). \tag{3.31}$$

The first order condition yields the optimal level of private human capital investments:

$$I_{it} = \frac{\gamma\omega\phi}{1+\gamma\omega\phi}(1-\tau)Y_{it-1}. \tag{3.32}$$

This level is the same as without public education, as public human capital investment does not affect the productivity of private investment. An explanation for the pattern is that private and public investments bring out different kinds of human capital. While public education investment, for example, contributes to more general knowledge, private investments may, for example, encourage soft skills. The consequence of differences in parental income, productivity of human capital investment, the earnings' return on human capital, and the degree of dynastic altruism are the same as in the case of a crowding-out effect of public education and private human capital investment.

If there is no effect of public education on private human capital investment, individual income in generation t arises - depending on parental optimization decision - as follows:

$$\log Y_{it} = \omega\phi \log(\frac{\gamma\omega\phi}{1+\gamma\omega\phi}) + \omega\phi \log((1-\tau)Y_{it-1} \cdot B_{it}) + \varphi G_{it} \tag{3.33}$$

Ignoring the inter-relation of state education investment and family background, intergenerational income elasticity is the same as in the absence of education policy. But taking into account the effect of a society's education policy—described by Equation (3.26)—for sufficiently small ν/N, intergenerational correlation of incomes arises as follows:[13]

$$\log Y_{it} \cong y_{nr} + \omega\phi(2 - \frac{\nu}{N}) \log Y_{it-1} + \varphi G_{it} \tag{3.34}$$
$$\text{with} \quad y_{nr} = \omega\phi \log(2(1-\tau) \cdot N \cdot \frac{\gamma\omega\phi}{1+\gamma\omega\phi}).$$

Thus, the long run intergenerational income elasticity is equivalent to:

$$\eta_{nr} = \frac{\omega\phi(2 - \frac{\nu}{N}) + g}{1 + \omega\phi(2 - \frac{\nu}{N})g}, \tag{3.35}$$

where the index nr stands for the scenario that no correlation between the level of private (public) human capital investment and the productivity of public (private) investment exists. As before, the income elasticity increases with greater heritability, higher productivity of human capital investment, higher earnings return on human capital, and less progressive state education investment.

Crowding-In Effect of Public and Private Human Capital Investments

If the transformation of human capital investment in human capital is identified by the following function:

$$H(I_{it}, B_{it}) = \phi \cdot \log I_{it} \cdot \log B_{it}, \tag{3.36}$$

the return of private human capital investment increases with public education expenditure.

The individual maximization problem with regard to the optimal level of private investment in the child's human capital is obtained by plugging in

[13]The derivation of this equation is in Appendix A.2.

Equations (3.13), (3.14), (3.15), and (3.36) in (3.17) and is given by:

$$\max_{I_{it}} U_{it-1} = \log((1-\tau)Y_{it-1} - I_{it}) + \gamma(\omega\phi \cdot \log I_{it} \cdot \log B_{it}). \tag{3.37}$$

The first order condition yields:

$$I_{it} = \frac{\gamma\omega\phi \log(B_{it})}{1+\gamma\omega\phi \log(B_{it})}(1-\tau)Y_{it-1}. \tag{3.38}$$

Public and private human capital investments are complements. Public education crowds-in private human capital investment, as the return of private investment increases with public education. An example of such private human capital investment is private lessons financed by parents; public investment would be the provision of public schools. The effects of the parameters Y_{it}, ϕ, ω, and γ are the same as for the other two possible interactions of public and private human capital investments. In sum, in any case the level of private investment in human capital increases with parental income, the productivity of human capital investments, the earnings return of human capital, and the degree of dynastic altruism. The magnitude of the effects, however, distinguish between the possible interactive effects. The greatest influence of the particular parameters on the optimal level of private investment is realized for the case of crowding-in of private human capital investment through public education.

Assuming there is a crowding-in effect of public and private human capital investments and supposing individual optimization, the relation between child income and parental income becomes:

$$\log Y_{it} = \omega\phi Q_{it} \log(\frac{\gamma\omega\phi Q_{it}}{1+\gamma\omega\phi Q_{it}}(1-\tau)) + \omega\phi Q_{it} \log Y_{it-1} + \varphi G_{it} \tag{3.39}$$
$$\text{with} \quad Q_{it} = \log(B_{it}).$$

Taking account of available parental income and gross income of the next generation, intergenerational income elasticity is:

$$\eta_{ci} = \frac{\omega\phi \log(B_t) + g}{1+\omega\phi \log(B_t) g} \tag{3.40}$$

with B_t the average education expenditures per capita. The determined intergenerational income elasticity ignores the potential inter-relation of state education investment and parental income, as occurs when education policy is described by (3.26). Unfortunately, because of formal limitations this lack cannot be resolved.

Summarizing, if the state invests in education, individual income will depend on hereditary factors, parental income, and in addition, on the state education investment received. Comparing Equations (3.27), (3.33), and (3.39), different interactions of public and private human capital investments can be associated with different aims pursued by different public education policies, such as those investigated in Weizsäcker (1999). If public and private human capital investments are substitutes, public education policy in general will underlie the aim of integration. Both other interactions vaguely pursue the aim of differentiation.

3.2.3 Impact of Public Education Policy

The consequences of public education policies on intergenerational income mobility depends on the interaction of public and private human capital investments. Whether education policy is successful in enhancing intergenerational income mobility for the three possible interactions is investigated.

Assuming a crowding-out of private through public human capital investment, intergenerational income elasticity and thus intergenerational correlation of income is smaller than without public education, as:

$$\eta_{na} > \eta_{co}.$$

Hence, supposing a crowding-out effect, the implementation of public education policy increases mobility (measured by $1 - \eta$). In that case, promoting greater equality of opportunity education policy entails less marked differences in private human capital investment across generations. Note, assuming a crowding-out effect of public and private human capital investment is interpretable as dominance of this effect over the other potential interactive effects, but does not mean that they cannot all co-exist.

If there is no effect of public education on private human capital investment and factoring in the correlation of state education investment and parental income, intergenerational income elasticity will be higher than without public education, as:

$$\eta_{nr} > \eta_{na}$$

for $N > \nu$ which is plausibly assumed. Consequently, in this case education policy reduces intergenerational income mobility. Similar to the case of performance schools in Weizsäcker (1999), the effect of public investment is linked to the particular dynasty and the available income of the previous generation of that dynasty. Hence, strengthening the effect of family background public education decreases income mobility in society.

Assuming a crowding-in effect of private and public human capital investments, for plausible value ranges of B_{it} ($\forall i \in I$) intergenerational income elasticity and thus intergenerational correlation of incomes is higher than without public education, as:

$$\eta_{ci} > \eta_{na}.$$

Note, η_{ci} ignores the inter-relation of state education investment and parental income. But if one would take the inter-relation of state education investment and parental income into account, the elasticity η_{ci} would be even higher, as the additional effect - which is not considered here - goes in the same direction. Consequentially, in the case of a crowding-in effect the intergenerational income elasticity η_{ci} is even higher than η_{nr}.

Summed up, for plausible value ranges, the comparison of the resultant intergenerational income elasticities yields:

$$\eta_{ci} > \eta_{nr} > \eta_{na} > \eta_{co}.$$

Only if public and private human capital investment are substitutes will the implementation of education policy or a raise of state education investment increase mobility. Even if state education investment does not have any influence on the return of private human capital investment, income elasticity increases with the implementation of such an education policy measure. In that case, the state cannot use public education policy to balance out advantages of children born into high-income families who receive higher private human capital investments than children born into low-income families. Achievable individual income is thus more strongly determined by individual income of the last generation than in the case of a crowding-out. Hence, unless private and public investment are substitutes, the state has less power to promote greater equality of opportunity. The correlation of income across generations and the disadvantages of children born into low-income families will be strongest if both kinds of investments complement each other. Consequently, in that case society is most immobile.

In addition, if there is a crowding-out effect of private through public human capital investment, basic income quantified by y_{co} will be highest. Whether it is higher or lower in the case of no relation between public and private investment than without public education depends on the magnitudes and relations of τ and N, respectively.

3.3 Implications

Education plays an important role for personal economic success. But, as it turns out, education policy does not ambiguously increase intergenerational income mobility. Weizsäcker (1999) shows that whether a rise in public education expenditure increases intergenerational income mobility depends on the aim of education policy. In contrast to the principle of differentiation, pursuing the aim of integration education policy always increases intergenerational income mobility.

Explicitly taking into account the individuals' response to public education policies, it reveals that the underlying interactive effect of public and private human capital investments is vital to the success of public education in enhancing intergenerational income mobility. Only if public education crowds out private human capital investment will the implementation of education policy increase intergenerational income mobility in society. Policy measures publicly funded, such as private tutoring for a child, reduces private lessons financed by parents. Thus, such measures promote greater equality of opportunity and increase intergenerational income mobility.

When deciding on the share of available income to invest in the child's education, in addition to public education, parents account for their own wealth as well as the expected return on human capital investment. The optimal level of private investment in the child's human capital increases with parental income and the earnings return on this investment. Hence, children of varying family background face inequality of opportunity. The implementation of education policy will contribute to more equal opportunities and higher intergenerational income mobility if the policy measure mitigates parental influence.

When public education does not affect private human capital investment, educational policy cannot counteract the advantage of children born into high-income families to receive more private human capital investment—even the opposite when public and private human capital investment are complements. Hence in these latter cases, the achievable income of the next generation depends more strongly on the income of the generation living today. As a consequence, mobility will be lower than if public and private human capital investment are substitutes and even lower than without education policy.

Even if parents' behavior is not affected by education policy measures, immobility increases with the implementation of such policies as the level of public investment depends on family background. In line with these results, in Weizsäcker (1999), implementing comprehensive schools that underlie the principle of integration unambiguously increases income mobility, as the public investment effect is independent of family background.

The strength of the economic parent-child connection and heritability of genetic basic endowment mainly determine intergenerational income mobility. When interpreting income in the model of Weizsäcker (1999) as logarithmic income, immobility measures—both intergenerational income elasticity and correlation—are identical in both models as in the long run income inequality is equal across generations. The influence of family background on economic success (β in Weizsäcker, 1999) corresponds to the earnings return on human capital investment, thus being formally precise on $\omega\phi$. Hence, a society is less mobile, the more productive human capital investment is and the higher the earnings return on human capital is. Since higher returns on private human capital investment lead to a greater dispersion of these investments, income inequality also increases with the productivity of human capital investment.

In addition to the return on human capital, heritability has a determining influence on mobility in society. If opportunities concerning private human capital investment are mostly equal, income immobility in society is mainly determined by heritability. According to Becker and Tomes (1986), if capital markets are perfect, parents will invest the same amount of human capital in their children and hence income mobility will only be determined by heritability of genetic basic endowment. Public education also influences mobility, depending on the progressivity of public human capital investment: the more progressive the public investment, the more mobile a society is.

The three possible interaction effects of private and public human capital investments may co-exist within a society. Whether the prevalence of one of the three potential interactions is dependent on the level of development of a country is an open and interesting question that requires further research. Conceivably, in developing countries in which there is no or little public education, policy measures tend to be such that private and public human capital investment are substitutes. In emerging countries in which public education is already provided, public and private human capital investments seem to complement each other. Hence, whether public education increases or decreases intergenerational income mobility may depend on the state of development: at a low level of development, income mobility increases with public education, whereas at intermediate levels implementing further education policy mobility decreases.

Chapter 4

Intergenerational Income Persistence in Germany: the Role of Education and Occupation

Since the late 1980s in the field of economics, empirical studies have enhanced the focus on intergenerational income mobility within societies (for international comparisons see, for example, Björklund and Jäntti 2000; Corak 2006). However, still little is known about the mechanism that underlies income persistence across generations. For example, questions about the importance of education and the education system in the process of income formation have so far mainly remained unanswered. Only recently earliest studies investigate potential reasons of income persistence within and across countries, especially for Great Britain and the United States (see, for example, Blanden et al., 2007, 2014; Hertz et al., 2007).

In analyzing the explanatory power of different pathway factors, such as education or occupation, this chapter addresses potential reasons of income immobility across generations in Germany. The empirical study proceeds according to the decomposition approach by Bowles and Gintis (2002), where the economic parent-child connection is decomposed into its direct and indirect components. The direct component of the parent-child connection is any factor not explained by the pathway factors included in the analysis. The indirect components describe the extent to which income persistence across generations is explained by individual characteristics such as education.

The main reasons for income persistence across generations in Germany are then compared with those in Great Britain and the United States. Here the results for Great Britain and the United States are taken from Blanden et al. (2014). For reasons of comparability the analysis includes the same potential pathway factors as in Blanden et al. (2014), which are education, occupation, labor market attachment, marital status, and health status. Showing similarities and differences between these countries, international comparison contributes to a deeper understanding of peculiarities within societies and thus possibly enables us to make a more target-oriented policy recommendation. Comparing Great Britain and the United States, Blanden et al. (2014) illustrate that the relationship underlying the intergenerational connection differs considerably: in the United States education has a relatively great importance as a pathway of intergenerational income persistence (basically because of high returns on education), while in Great Britain occupation is mainly responsible for economic persistence across generations.

4.1 Income Persistence across Generations

In this section, the aim is to estimate the existing intergenerational income (im)mobility in Germany in order to then investigate the mechanisms that underlie income persistence across generations in Section 4.2. Starting with theoretical insights into intergenerational income mobility, the theoretical work in Chapter 3 is connected to the empirical investigation in this chapter.

4.1.1 Theoretical Background

The aim of the empirical investigation in this chapter is (i) to understand the processes that underlie the transmission of economic position from one generation to the next in Germany and (ii) to highlight similarities and differences between the three nations Germany, Great Britain, and the United States. In doing this, the empirical work in this chapter is connected to the theoretical model in Chapter 3: Again, dynastic altruism is assumed. Consequently, parents benefit from their own consumption and the consumption level (and economic status, respectively) of their child in adulthood. Both innate abilities and the value of received human capital investment have a determining influence on economic success and thus individual earnings. The received level of private human capital investment in turn hinges on the child's skills and abilities, as well as on family background: as shown in detail in Chapter 3, both factors enhance private human capital investment.

With regard to international differences in intergenerational income mobility, insights are gained from the theoretical literature involving the papers of Becker and Tomes (1986), Weizsäcker (1999), Solon (2004), and the contribution in

Chapter 3. Accordingly, country A appears to be less mobile than country B if in country A:

(i) heritability is higher,

(ii) human capital investment is more productive,

(iii) the return of human capital is higher,

(iv) public human capital investment is less progressive,

(v) in contrast to country B, public education does not predominantly crowd out private human capital investment,

(vi) the capital market is less smoothly functioning,

(vii) individual preferences concerning the levels of education and occupation are strongly dependent on parental preferences,

(viii) the quality of schooling within society displays large differences, and/or

(ix) education levels are highly heterogeneous.

When later comparing the relationship which underlies the intergenerational economic connection in the three nations Germany, Great Britain, and the United States, the role played by the return on human capital and the earnings return to human capital investment are especially delved into.

4.1.2 Immobility of Income across Generations

The intergenerational connection between parent and child income, and hence income persistence across generations, is commonly specified by either the intergenerational income elasticity or the correlation of incomes across generations. Both of these two standard approaches are included in the theory-based considerations in Chapter 3. In what follows, for both approaches a log-linear relationship of parent-child incomes is assumed.[1] Estimation of the intergenerational immobility by quantifying the intergenerational income elas-

[1]This is a common assumption in the empirical literature on intergenerational income mobility. All of the cited empirical studies suppose such a log-linear relation of parent-child incomes.

ticity (denoted by β) takes the following (simplified) regression as a basis:

$$\log Y_i^C = \alpha + \beta \log Y_i^P + \epsilon. \tag{4.1}$$

Index i marks a specific family dynasty, C stands for the child generation and P for the parent generation. Accordingly, $\log Y_i^C$ is the logarithmic life-time income (or earning) of the child of dynasty i. The parameter α corresponds to the average logarithmic income (or earning) in the child generation and ϵ marks the error term. The income elasticity β determines the influence of parental income on the child's economic success. Thus, $1 - \beta$ quantifies the degree of income mobility in society. The value range of β lies between zero and one: $\beta = 1$ reflects a completely immobile society with each individual staying in the same income class as its ancestors; $\beta = 0$ marks a completely mobile society. The intergenerational income elasticity is described by:

$$\beta = \frac{Cov(\log Y_i^P, \log Y_i^C)}{\sigma_P^2},$$

whereas income correlation across generations (denoted by ρ) is defined by:

$$\rho = \frac{Cov(\log Y_i^P, \log Y_i^C)}{\sigma_P \cdot \sigma_C}.$$

Here σ_P (σ_C) reflects the standard deviation of income in the parent (child) generation and σ_P^2 (σ_C^2) the respective variance of income. In contrast to estimates of β, measuring the income correlation ρ adjusts for differences in income variances between the two generations. Formally, the link between the two measures is as follows:

$$\rho = \beta \cdot \frac{\sigma_P}{\sigma_C}.$$

The correlation measure allows for different levels of inequality between generations and thus changes in inequality across generations, while the elasticity measure does not. Hence, the two measures will be identical if income inequality remains the same across generations. If however income inequality increases, the estimated intergenerational income elasticity will be higher than the corresponding income correlation.

Intergenerational Income Immobility in Germany

Applying both the elasticity and the correlation measure, the degree of intergenerational income immobility in Germany is estimated. For this purpose data is used from the *German Socio-Economic Panel* (SOEP)[2], a longitudinal panel survey data source in Germany. Drawing on such longitudinal panel data sources is standard in empirical research on intergenerational income mobility (for this, see Solon, 1992; Zimmerman, 1992). Investigating the economic parent-child link, Blanden et al. (2014) apply the 1970 *British Cohort Study* (BCS) for Great Britain and the *Panel Study of Income Dynamics* (PSID) for the United States, both also prominent longitudinal panel survey data sources.

In order to meaningfully compare the three nations,[3] the sample used for Germany should meet the same requirements as the samples for Great Britain and the United States in Blanden et al. (2014), but without sacrificing data quality. In addition, the same measures for economic status should be used. Thus, as measure of a child's economic background, parental income is taken into account, whereas earnings are considered as a measure of the economic success of the child. To use parental income as a measure of economic background is adequate, as it includes transfers which definitely are important for parental resources. According to Björklund and Jäntti (2000) more frequently earnings are used as a measure of economic success for both parents and children.[4]

Similar to Blanden et al. (2014), my sample only includes individuals that participate in the SOEP survey, both as child in the 10-16 age group and as young adult in the 29-34 age group. Requiring information about parental income in childhood (at child age between 10 and 16) and child earnings in young-adult life (at the 29-34 age group), all individuals are included in the sample who report at least once on parental income and child earnings at the relevant age groups, hence maximizing the sample size. The resulting sample set consists of 1,211 parent-child pairs, including 617 sons and 594 daughters.

[2]Data from the German Socio-Economic Panel used in the subsequent empirical research are provided by the German Institute for Economic Research (DIW Berlin).

[3]When in Section 4.2 reasons for intergenerational persistence of income are analyzed, international comparison is important in order to generate robust results.

[4]The British data using BCS do not include separate information on parental earnings.

Three main methodological problems may arise when estimating income persistence across generations (by β and ρ):[5] (i) unrepresentative samples, (ii) life-cycle bias, and (iii) measurement error.[6] The problem of unrepresentative samples is not relevant in the empirical analysis, as the data from the German SOEP are based on a nationally representative sample. Second, lifetime income is necessary to precisely quantify intergenerational income mobility within a society and to avoid life-cycle bias. As such data are not available, for Germany or any other country, approximate income observations are used over a time period, which is as long as possible in order to minimize the potential life-cycle bias. Third, in classical linear models measurement error of dependent variables, such as child earnings, are included in the error term ϵ_i, but measurement error in the independent variable (parental income) results in an underestimation of β. Hence, allowing for income observation over a time period that is as long as possible and taking into account the mean of parental income and the child's earning, in addition minimizes the bias that occurs because of measurement error. In the dataset used, measurement error is diminished by using average measure of parental income over a maximal seven-year period and children's earnings over a maximal five-year period. Another possible cause of systematic underestimation of the coefficient β is the observation of incomes at different ages. For this reason control variables are included for the average and quadratic average age of each individual in the sample.

Most of the international evidence considers father-son pairs for estimating intergenerational income mobility (and earnings mobility, respectively). This is due to less suitable data being available for women. Even nowadays women still earn less than men in comparable occupational position. Only a few decades ago the model of the man as sole bread-winner was prevailing in Germany.

[5]In line with most of the literature on intergenerational mobility the empirical research applies a linear model of intergenerational persistence, but recent studies—for example, Björklund, Roine, and Waldenström (2012); Bratsberg et al. (2007); Hirvonen (2010)—doubt the adequacy of these linear models demonstrating the potential importance of non-linearity: first, it is questionable whether the observations provided in the German sample are sufficient to adequately estimate the correlation considering the possibility of non-linearity. Second, even if the effect of parental background is not necessarily the same over the entire earnings distribution, average measures of persistence will have as advantage to be easily interpretable.

[6]For a detailed discussion of methodological problems see, for example, Blanden (2009).

Table 4.1: Intergenerational Income Persistence - Germany

Elasticity (β)	Correlation (ρ)
0.276***	0.189***
(0.060)	(0.036)

Significance level: *** < 0.01.

When dealing with earning data, in young adult age those data may even be more biased for women, as the time to start a family includes this period. Hence, the main focus is on sons and daughters represent the control group.

The German sample includes 617 sons, designated below as men. These men earn on average €28,956 per year (with €16,931 being the standard deviation). The average age at which earnings are observed is 30.8 years. Parental income when those men were between 10 and 16 years old is on average €34,939 per year (with a standard deviation of €16,060). These parents had an average age of 43.4 years.[7]

For German men, the result of the OLS regression of Equation (4.1) is shown in Table 4.1. The intergenerational income elasticity is highly significant, amounting to about 0.28. Thus, an increase in parental income by one percent on average yield a 0.28 percentage increase in the child's earnings. It is highly significant that income correlation is only about 0.19. Thus, large differences between the elasticity and the correlation measure indicate rapid growth of earnings inequality in Germany over the observed period.

For German women, the descriptive statistics and the resulting intergenerational income immobility are shown respectively in Tables B.1 and B.2 in Appendix B. The 594 women of the German sample are on average of the same age as men and have nearly the same parental background (on average €34,797 per year), but average earnings considerably distinguish between the genders: of the same age, women earn on average €10,546 less per year than men.[8] Despite all the differences between the genders, intergenerational income elasticity is nearly the same, only marginally higher for women than for men. Income correlation paints a different picture: according to the correlation measure,

[7]The descriptive statistics of the men cohort is shown in Table 4.4. Monetary values for Germany are given in year 2000 euros.

[8]This illustrates the problems with women's data mentioned above.

Table 4.2: Intergenerational Income Persistence - Great Britain and the United States

	Great Britain	United States
Elasticity (β)	0.294***	0.385***
	(0.017)	(0.047)
Correlation (ρ)	0.283***	0.301***
	(0.017)	(0.037)

Significance level: *** < 0.01.
These estimation results for both Great Britain and the United States are taken from Blanden et al. (2014).

mobility is much higher for women (0.10) than for men (0.19). Comparing β and ρ for both women and men indicates a larger increase in earning inequality for women than for men in Germany. But, as outlined above, women's data, and thus the results for women, should be handled with care.

Intergenerational Income Immobility in International Comparison

Comparing intergenerational mobility that exists in Germany, Great Britain, and the United States (for this, see Tables 4.1 and 4.2), according to both measures, Germany tends to be the most mobile of the three nations, followed by Great Britain with an income elasticity of about 0.29 and income correlation valued at 0.28. Hence, the United States—with an income elasticity of 0.39 and an income correlation of 0.30—has the highest income persistence across generations. All the results are highly significant. Showing international differences, the elasticity and the correlation measure obtain relatively similar results for Great Britain, which is not the case for Germany and the United States. In both of the latter nations, correlation is substantially smaller than the elasticity, thus indicating a rapid growth of earnings inequality in those nations for the observed period.

Comparing the three countries, the descriptive statistics (presented in Table B.10 in Appendix B) highlight that mean income and earnings are highest in the United States; Germany comes in second. In both generations inequality is highest in the United States, whereas Germany indicates the lowest level of inequality. Quantifying inequality by the ratio of the standard deviation of earnings and average earnings, in the child generation inequality is about 0.88

in the United States, 0.66 in Great Britain and 0.58 in Germany. Germany, hence, seems to be both the most mobile and the most equal of the three nations.

4.2 Intergenerational Transmission of Income Inequality

The empirical analysis in this section aims to locate potential channels through which economic advantage and disadvantage are passed across generations. In quantifying the explanatory power of various pathways, the subsequent study incorporates education, occupation, labor market attachment, marital status, and health status as potential pathways for the intergenerational transmission of income inequality. The findings for Germany are then compared to those for Great Britain and the United States as measured by Blanden et al. (2014).

4.2.1 Decomposition of Intergenerational Income Persistence

The influence of family background on children's earnings operates through various channels. In order to discern the mechanisms that underlie income persistence, the intergenerational income elasticity β is decomposed into its direct and indirect components by applying the decomposition approach of Bowles and Gintis (2002). The indirect components measure the extent to which persistence across generations is transmitted by certain characteristics, such as education or occupation. When one considers, for example, education as a pathway of intergenerational transmission, the indirect component comprises (i) the effect of parental income on the child's educational attainment and (ii) the influence of education on economic success—thus its monetary value. The direct component is the effect of parental income on the child's economic success not explained by the pathway factors included in the analysis.

According to the theory-based analysis in Chapter 3, the child's status depends on his or her received human capital investment, which in turn increases with parental income and his or her ability. Combining empirical research with the theory of intergenerational mobility, in the decomposition approach the economic parent-child connection is determined by the influence of parental income on the level of investment in, for example, education and the return on these investment. Hence, parental income and the child's earnings are linked through the child's human capital.

The decomposition approach is illustrated, assuming only two potential channels, namely education and occupation, to which persistence of income are passed across generations. When presenting the approach, for simplicity the two pathway variables are imagined to be continuous variables. But actually, in the empirical study both education and occupation are categorical variables.[9] Aiming to quantify the explanatory power of different pathway factors as well as their possible interaction, the decomposition of intergenerational income immobility is separated into various sequential analyses. Here potential pathway variables are added to the model in the order in which they occur in the aging process. This takes into account the fact that characteristics which are present at younger ages influence those reflecting status at older ages. Hence, education is first considered in a sequential analysis and then a further sequential analysis additionally incorporates the pathway occupation. Implicitly, it is thus assumed that individual educational achievement is independent of occupation (but not vice versa). Even though conceivably some individuals determine educational achievements dependent on their occupational aim, at the country level this endogeneity problem is negligible. In addition, the endogeneity problem is mitigated by a wide-ranging clustering of occupation levels (which is done in the empirical research).

In the first sequential analysis, including only education, the link between education and parental income is initially estimated using the following regression:

$$Ed_i^C = \alpha_{Ed} + \lambda_{Ed} \log Y_i^P + e_{1i}, \tag{4.2}$$

[9]Following the example of Blanden et al. (2014), this procedure provides a clear overview of the main features of the approach. Later, presenting the decomposition approach for education as a categorical variable, shows the exact formal procedure.

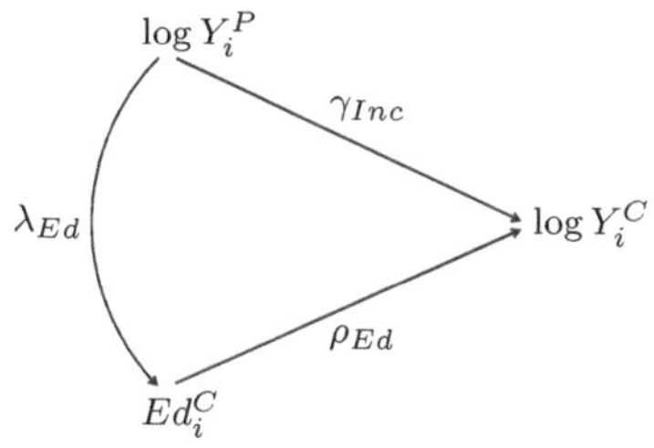

Figure 4.1: Decomposition of Income Immobility

where Ed_i^C is the child's achieved level of education and the coefficient λ_{Ed} measures the influence of parental income on the pathway education. Then the connection between the child's earning and both its educational achievement and parental income is estimated with:

$$\log Y_i^C = \omega_1 + \rho_{Ed} Ed_i^C + \gamma_{Inc} \log Y_i^P + v_{1i}, \tag{4.3}$$

where ρ_{Ed} specifies the earnings return on education and γ_{Inc} the correlation of incomes across generations not explained by education. Combining Equations (4.2) and (4.3) yields:

$$\log Y_i^C = \omega_1 + \rho_{Ed}\alpha_{Ed} + (\rho_{Ed}\lambda_{Ed} + \gamma_{Inc}) \log Y_i^P + \rho_{Ed} e_{1i} + v_{1i},$$

thus the intergenerational income elasticity derived by regression equation (4.1) is decomposed into:

$$\beta = \rho_{Ed}\lambda_{Ed} + \gamma_{Inc}. \tag{4.4}$$

The first term of Equation (4.4), $\rho_{Ed}\lambda_{Ed}$, indicates the part of total β to which intergenerational persistence is transmitted through education. This indirect component of β is specified by the strength of both the relationship between parental income and the pathway factor and the relationship between the pathway factor and its earning payoff. The second term determines the non-pathway effect and thus the direct component of β not explained by education. Only including the pathway education, Figure 4.1 graphically presents the intergenerational relations between parental income, educational achievement, and the child's earnings.[10]

In the second sequential analysis, in addition to educational achievement, the pathway factor occupation is added to the model. Again, the link between the pathway variables and parental income is estimated. In the case of occupation, this includes the estimation of the following regression equation:

$$Occ_i^C = \alpha_{Occ} + \lambda_{Occ} \log Y_i^P + e_{2i}, \tag{4.5}$$

where Occ_i^C is the child's occupation and the coefficient λ_{Occ} measures the influence of parental income on the pathway occupation. The connection between the child's earnings and both pathway factors, education and occupation, as well as parental income is then estimated using:

$$\log Y_i^C = \omega_2 + \gamma_{Ed} Ed_i^C + \gamma_{Occ} Occ_i^C + \gamma_{Inc} \log Y_i^P + v_{2i}, \tag{4.6}$$

where γ_{Occ} (γ_{Ed}) marks the earnings return to occupation (education).[11] The estimated return to each pathway variable is conditional on the other variables considered. Using the regression equations (4.2), (4.5), and (4.6), the decomposition of β becomes:

$$\beta = \lambda_{Ed}\gamma_{Ed} + \lambda_{Occ}\gamma_{Occ} + \gamma_{Inc}. \tag{4.7}$$

The first term of Equation (4.7) is the component of β which is transmitted through education. The component stated by the second term, $\lambda_{Occ}\gamma_{Occ}$, is the part of total β which is explained by the pathway factor occupation. Finally, the third term is the part of total β which can neither be explained by education nor occupation.

Reiterating, by ordering the pathway factors in the same way as they occur in the aging process, the analysis allows for the fact that variables that occur earlier in the aging process influence those which occur later. As some of the effect of earlier pathways is transmitted through pathways reflecting status at older ages, the part of total β that is explained by earlier pathway variables

[10] Here the graphical presentation follows the example of Bowles and Gintis (2002).

[11] Generally, below λ measures the influence of parental income on a pathway factor (which is specified via index) and γ indicates the earnings return to the respective pathway factor.

decreases when later pathway variables are added into the model. Thus in the above example the part of total β that is explained by education becomes significantly smaller when occupation is included. Here, $(\lambda_{Ed}\rho_{Ed} - \lambda_{Ed}\gamma_{Ed})$ measures the extent to which the influence of education is transmitted through occupation.

In the second sequential analysis, intergenerational income elasticity is decomposed into a direct effect and its indirect effects through education and occupation by estimating (4.2), (4.5), and (4.6). In order to consistently estimate the coefficients on education and occupation, γ_{Ed} and γ_{Occ}, in Equation (4.6) the corresponding error term v_{2i} must be uncorrelated with both e_{1i} (in Equation (4.2)) and e_{2i} (in Equation (4.5)).[12] In reality this assumption is rather doubtful (for this, see Hirvonen (2010), for example). Factors such as ability are likely to play a role in the level of earnings, the attained education level, and occupational choice, thus inducing estimation bias: if v_{2i} and e_{1i} are positively correlated, the importance of education in intergenerational transmission is overestimated. In addition, if $Cov(e_{1i}, v_{2i}) > Cov(e_{2i}, v_{2i})$, the relative role of education is overestimated compared to the role played by occupation.[13] According to Hirvonen (2010) however, the appearing problem of bias can be diminished by including more pathway variables. With regard to cross-national differences, results will be robust if correlations between v_{2i}, e_{1i}, and e_{2i} have the same magnitude across nations. Hence, as there is no reason why this cannot be assumed for the three nations Germany, Great Britain, and the United States, the results of the international comparison are robust. For completeness the model assumes constant returns to the pathway variables and their independence from parental income.

4.2.2 Pathways of Intergenerational Transmission

The empirical analysis considers education, occupation, labor market attachment, marital status, and health status as potential pathways through which the persistence of income inequality are passed across generations. Obviously, further potential pathway factors are conceivable to be partially responsible for the intergenerational transmission of income inequality. For example, neither

[12] As stated by Blanden et al. (2014).
[13] For a more detailed discussion about the emerging problems see Blanden et al. (2014).

cognitive nor non-cognitive abilities are included in the empirical estimation. First, in particular with regard to cognitive and non-cognitive abilities, Blanden et al. (2007) show that once education is included most effects of such abilities are minimized. Second, the selection of the pathway factors is in accordance with Blanden et al. (2014) in order to meaningfully compare the results for Germany with those for Great Britain and the United States. This is important in terms of robustness of the results. For reasons of comparability, not only the same pathway factors are used as in the empirical investigation of Blanden et al. (2014), but also the same categorization of those pathway variables. If possible the categorization of the variables will be based on international standard classification.

First, concerning education four levels of educational achievement are distinguished based on the International Standard Classification of Education (ISCED): (i) "less than high school graduation", (ii) "high school graduation", (iii) "attending college", and (iv) "college graduation". With regard to the German education system, Table 4.3 displays German educational attainment associated with the four categories. In each category all individuals are incorporated with the specific educational attainment.

Based on these four categories, three categorical variables are created defined by: "at least high school", "at least some college", and "completed college". The variable "completed college", denoted by $Ed3$, ("at least some college"—denoted by $Ed2$) takes the value one for individuals with educational attainment equal to or higher than college graduation (college attendance) and zero for all others. The variable "at least high school"—denoted by $Ed1$—is one for individuals with educational attainment equal or higher than high school graduation and zero for all others. The reference level for "at least high school" is thus "less than high school graduation". In order to avoid ambiguity arising when estimating the relationship between parental income and the middle categories of educational attainment (Equation (4.2)), no exclusive dummies in categorical variables are used. Otherwise ambiguity would appear since, for example, those who attend college are well educated compared to those with high school graduation or lower educational attainment, but poorly educated compared to those who graduate from college.

Table 4.3: Educational Attainment according to the German Education System

"less than high school graduation"	- "Hauptschul-/Realschulabschluss"
"high school graduation"	- "Fachhochschulreife/Hochschulreife; ohne beruflichen Abschluss" - "Abschluss einer Lehrausbildung" - "Abschluss des Vorbereitungsdienstes für den mittleren Dienst in der öffentlichen Verwaltung"
"attending college"	- "Fachhochschulreife/Hochschulreife und Abschluss einer Lehrausbildung"
"college graduation"	- "Hochschul-/Fachhochschulabschluss" - "Meister-/Technikerausbildung, Verwaltungsfachhochschulabschluss" - "Promotion/Habilitation"

For the classification of German educational attainments to the ISCED see, for example, CESifo (2014).

In the German sample educational attainment is measured at the age of 30. If educational attainment is not available at this age, it will be observed at younger ages (with 22 being the lowest accepted age). Summed up, the study refers back to the latest information about educational attainment of each child in the 22 to 30 age group.

By decomposing intergenerational income immobility, the application of the categorical variables defined above necessitates estimation of the link between parental income and education for each variable. Hence, the formerly indicated regression equation (4.2) exactly involves the following three regression equations:

$$Ed1_i^C = \alpha_{Ed1} + \lambda_{Ed1} \log Y_i^P + e_{Ed1,i}, \tag{4.8}$$

$$Ed2_i^C = \alpha_{Ed2} + \lambda_{Ed2} \log Y_i^P + e_{Ed2,i}, \tag{4.9}$$

$$Ed3_i^C = \alpha_{Ed3} + \lambda_{Ed3} \log Y_i^P + e_{Ed3,i}. \tag{4.10}$$

When quantifying the effect of educational attainment on child earnings, the effect is estimated separately for the three variables $Ed1$, $Ed2$, and $Ed3$. Thus, including only education as pathway factor, for example, regression equation (4.3) turns into:[14]

$$\log Y_i^C = \omega_1 + \gamma_{Ed1} Ed1_i^C + \gamma_{Ed2} Ed2_i^C + \gamma_{Ed3} Ed3_i^C + \gamma_{Inc} \log Y_i^P + v_{1i}. \tag{4.11}$$

In that case, the decomposition of β becomes:

$$\beta = \lambda_{Ed1}\gamma_{Ed1} + \lambda_{Ed2}\gamma_{Ed2} + \lambda_{Ed3}\gamma_{Ed3} + \gamma_{Inc}.$$

The first three terms comprise the part of β explained by education. The fourth term indicates the part of β not explained by education, thus indicating the direct effect of family background.

Second, categorizing occupational achievement, Blanden et al. (2014) use the eight-category version of the National Statistics Socio-Economic Classification (NS-SEC) system consisting of:

(i) "higher managerial and professional occupation",

(ii) "lower managerial and professional occupation",

(iii) "intermediate occupation",

(iv) "small employers or self-employed",

(v) "lower supervisory and technical occupation",

(vi) "semi-routine occupation",

(vii) "routine occupation", and

(viii) "missing values".

This classification system is common and widely used in Great Briatin in both official statistics and academic research and the British data are coded accord-

[14] Including other pathway factors does not change this procedure. Following the same pattern for the pathway factor occupation, all categorical variables summarizing occupational achievement are included when measuring the importance of this pathway.

ing to this classification.[15] For reasons of comparability, the NS-SEC system is applied to German data. In addition, in the case of Germany the use of the NS-SEC system is justified, as this system is closely related to the European Socio-economic Classification (ESeC) with the only difference being that the NS-SEC system sums up two categories of the ESeC.[16] The SOEP data set provides occupational information that is categorized according to the four-digit version of the International Standard Classification of Occupation (ISCO). In order to apply the NS-SEC categorization to German data, the ISCO variables are transformed into the ESeC categorization. Then, using these new variables, occupational dummy variables are generated according to the NS-SEC system.

As for the pathway education, occupational achievement enters the analysis as categorical variables. For this purpose, based on the eight-category NS-SEC system six dummy variables are generated defined as follows:

$Occ1$ - "at least semi-routine occupation",

$Occ2$ - "at least lower supervisory and technical occupation",

$Occ3$ - "at least small employers or self-employed",

$Occ4$ - "at least intermediate occupation",

$Occ5$ - "at least lower managerial and professional occupation", and

$Occ6$ - "higher managerial and professional occupation".

Each of these dummy variables takes the value one for individuals whose occupation level is equal or above the relevant level and zero for all others. The dummy for the highest occupation level, for example, equals one for those individuals with higher managerial and professional occupation. In interpreting the results, the coefficient estimate of the highest occupation level thus indicates the marginal effect of this occupation level compared to the next lower level. The lowest level of occupation that is considered in the analysis is denoted by $Occ1$ and takes the value one for individuals with semi-routine occupation or higher occupational levels and zero for all others. The reference group for

[15] For the United States, data about occupational status are transformed into this classification system.

[16] According to the (nine-category) ESeC, the NS-SEC category "small employers and self-employed" is separated for the agricultural and non-agricultural sector.

this dummy is those individuals with routine occupations. Individual level of occupation is measured at both the age of 30 and the age of 34. If for these two ages no information about occupational achievement is available, the individual occupational level will be considered for the closest younger age above 25 and 31, respectively.

Third, labor market attachment is measured in the 22 to 25 age group and in the 26 to 29 age group. For both age groups, individual attachment to the labor market is indicated in two ways: (i) by the percent of years in which the child is not primarily active in the labor market nor in school and (ii) by the percent of years in which the child is employed in a full-time position or in training. The former variable includes all years in which the annual work hours of an individual are less than 500 and the individual is neither in school nor in training. The latter variable incorporates those years in which either annual work hours are at least 1500 or the individual is at school or in training.

Fourth, marital status is measured for two age groups entering the analysis for both ages as a dummy variable. The first dummy equals one for those individuals who married before or at the age of 22 and zero for all others. The second dummy variable indicates whether individuals are married before or at the age of 30 taking the value one if they are married and zero if they are not.

Finally, the self-rated health status is taken into account. The SOEP survey asks its participants about their health status where they can choose between the levels (i) excellent, (ii) very good, (iii) good, (iv) fair, and (v) poor. On the basis of this self-rated health status at the age of 30 (or if not available at this age, at younger ages above 22), two dummy variables are generated: the first dummy variable takes the value one for those whose reported health status is excellent and zero for all others. The second dummy variable equals one for all those with fair or poor health and zero for all others. Accordingly, the reference group are those with either very good or good health reported.

Table 4.4 shows the descriptive statistics for the main variables for the men cohort. Almost 82 percent at least graduate from high school, but only 38 percent attend college, of which nearly 80 percent graduate. In absolute terms, almost 30 percent of the participants graduate from college. The share of men in full-time positions increases with age (from 68 percent to 75 percent) and

Table 4.4: Descriptive Statistics for Main Variables (German Men)

Average parental income at 10 and 16	34,939
(standard deviation)	(16,060)
Average sons' earnings at 30 and 34	28,956
(standard deviation)	(16,931)
Average parental age	43.4
Average sons' age	30.8
At least high school graduate	81.9%
At least some college	38.0%
Graduate college/ Degree	29.9%
Education missing	6.6%
Married at age 22 or less	5.2%
Missing married at 22	2.6%
Ages 22-25 No labor/ education	17.6%
Ages 22-25 Full-time work/ education	67.8%
Ages 26-29 No labor/ education	12.7%
Ages 26-29 Full-time work/ education	74.9%
Missing labor market info	0.6%
Married at 30	34.7%
Missing married at 30	6.2%
Health excellent at 30	15.7%
Health poor plus fair at 30	4.8%
Health missing at 30	6.2%
Semi-routine occupation or higher at 30	85.4%
Lower supervisory and technical occupation or higher at 30	57.6%
Small employers and self-employed or higher at 30	52.1%
Intermediate occupation or higher at 30	46.1%
Lower managerial and professional or higher at 30	37.2%
Higher managerial and professional at 30	19.1%
Missing occupation at 30	16.7%
Semi-routine occupation or higher at 34	65.3%
Lower supervisory and technical occupation or higher at 34	46.9%
Small employers and self-employed or higher at 34	42.8%
Intermediate occupation or higher at 34	37.9%
Lower managerial and professional or higher at 34	31.9%
Higher managerial and professional at 34	17.0%
Missing occupation at 34	10.2%

Notes: Monetary values for Germany are given in year 2000 euros. Means of the variables are only the means of observations not missing. As appropriate, missing values are replaced with these mean values in the empirical analysis.

those without work decreases (from 18 percent to 13 percent). At the age of 22 only 5 percent of the men are married, at the age of 30 the percentage is almost 35 percent. 15.7 percent of the cohort stated that they are in excellent health and only 4.8 percent are in poor or fair condition. Finally, at age 30, 85 percent of men have at least a semi-routine occupation, more than 50 percent of the cohort reach at least the occupation level equal to the "small employers and self-employed" category and almost 20 percent achieve the highest occupational level. Comparing the occupational achievements at the age of 30 and 34, it becomes obvious that the percentage of men achieving at least a certain level of occupation is lower at higher ages than when they are younger. This rather implausible observation is due to the fact that less data is available for the age of 34.[17] Thus, occupational information for men at older ages should be handled with care.

4.2.3 Intergenerational Transmission

After indicating the potential pathways of intergenerational transmission of income inequality, the explanatory power of those pathways are quantified for the case of Germany. Afterwards similarities and differences are revealed in intergenerational transmission between Germany, Great Britain, and the United States.

Intergenerational Transmission of Income Inequality in Germany

Estimating the significance of pathway factors in the intergenerational transmission of income immobility, the method of measurement is as follows: for each pathway factor that is included in the sequential analysis the link between the pathway factor and parental income is estimated—for example, for education by the regression equations (4.8) - (4.10). Then an extended version of regression equation (4.1) is estimated, including the respective pathway factors as independent variables. For the education-only model, for example, the regression equation turns into Equation (4.11). Finally, the part and the percent of total β explained by the pathway factors included in the model are calcu-

[17]The lower missing value at age 34 compared to that at age 30 only suggests that the occupation level is missing for 10 percent of men for which data are available at the age of 34, while for 16.7 percent of men for which data are available at the age of 30 information about occupational achievement is missing.

lated. When estimating the regression equations and afterwards determining the share to which intergenerational immobility is explained by the pathway factors, the bootstrapping method is used (with 1000 replications).

Table 4.5 shows the results of the sequential decomposition approach for German men. As pathway factors are taken into account in the order in which they occur in the aging process, the first sequential analysis only considers education as pathway of intergenerational transmission; its results are presented in column (1). In the second sequential analysis, highlighted in column (2), the pathway factors early marriage (that is marital status at the age of 22) and labor market attachment in the 22-25 age group are additionally taken into account. The third sequential analysis incorporates education, early marriage, labor market attachment in both the 22-25 and the 26-29 age group, marital status, reported health status, and occupation, the latter three at the age of 30. The results of the third sequential analysis are shown in column (3). Finally, in the fourth sequential analysis, column (4), occupation at the age of 34 is additionally included into the model.

Reiterating, for German men the intergenerational income elasticity β is highly significant and amounts to 0.276 as presented in the last row of Table 4.5. Solely including education as a potential pathway, it is accountable for 0.062 of total β (on a significance level below 1%). In the education-only model, this pathway explains 22.6 percent of total β and 78.9 percent remains unexplained. Incorporating early marriage and labor market attachment in the 22-25 age group does not offer much additional explanation of the existing intergenerational income immobility; still about 75 percent of total β remains unexplained. In general, marital status, health status as well as labor market attachment for both the 22-25 and the 26-29 age group add little explanation of income persistence across generations. Most important for the intergenerational transmission of income inequality in Germany is education, with occupational achievement at the age of 30 coming in second. Independent of the sequential analysis, both the part of β that remains unexplained and the part of β that is explained in total by the pathway factors included are significant. The same holds for the effect of education, whereas the effect of no other pathway factor is significant. Comparing the first three sequential analyses, the explained component of the intergenerational income elasticity that

Table 4.5: Sequential Decomposition - Germany

Explained components of total β	(1) Part of total β	(1) Percent of total β	(2) Part of total β	(2) Percent of total β	(3) Part of total β	(3) Percent of total β	(4) Part of total β	(4) Percent of total β
Education	0.062** (0.028)	22.6% (31.1)	0.078*** (0.030)	28.2% (33.7)	0.075*** (0.026)	27.2% (42.8)	0.068** (0.027)	24.5% (489.7)
Early marriage			−0.007 (0.008)	−2.5% (4.7)	−0.005 (0.005)	−1.9% (4.3)	−0.005 (0.006)	−1.9% (121.2)
Labor market attachment, ages 22-25			0.003 (0.026)	1.0% (31.4)	−0.002 (0.016)	−0.7% (34.6)	0.003 (0.016)	0.9% (175.7)
Labor market attachment, ages 26-29					0.016 (0.025)	5.8% (31.0)	0.017 (0.026)	6.1% (105.1)
Marriage and health at 30					−0.008 (0.015)	−2.7% (15.3)	−0.008 (0.015)	−3.0% (139.3)
Occupation at age 30					0.045 (0.036)	16.3% (44.0)	0.034 (0.039)	12.3% (142.5)
Occupation at age 34							−0.001 (0.023)	−0.3% (124.5)
Missing values	−0.004 (0.014)	−1.4% (21.5)	−0.005 (0.010)	−1.8% (9.3)	0.017 (0.025)	6.0% (43.7)	0.016 (0.025)	6.0% (236.0)
Explained component of β	0.062** (0.028)	22.6% (31.1)	0.074* (0.041)	26.7% (43.2)	0.121** (0.057)	43.9% (52.0)	0.102* (0.059)	36.8% (253.1)
Unexplained component of β	0.218* (0.105)	78.9% (31.7)	0.207** (0.099)	75.1% (39.6)	0.138 (0.095)	50.1% (49.2)	0.158 (0.099)	57.2% (141.2)
Total β	0.276***		0.276***		0.276***		0.276***	

Significance levels: *** < 0.01, ** < 0.05, and * < 0.1.

exists in Germany increases with the pathway factors included in the model. Disregarding the fourth sequential analysis is justified, as occupation at the age of 34 lacks quality and validity since less data is available for men at this age. Furthermore, as the two occupational variables are at least collinear to some extent, difficulties may arise concerning the differentiation of the two effects.

In summary, up to nearly 44 percent of intergenerational income elasticity is attributed to the pathway factors that are included in the empirical analysis, from which education has the greatest importance (ranging from 22.6 to 28.2 percent); occupation at the age of 30 (with about 16 percent) comes in second. Here, at least one-fifth of the intergenerational income immobility is transmitted through education. Occupation adds additional explanations of β by around 15 percent, leading to about 40 percent of the existing intergenerational immobility that is explained in total. When including occupation as a pathway, the explanatory power of education decreases. Thus as expected, the pathway occupation tends to absorb explanatory power that had before been ascribed to education. The results remain unaffected when replacing parental with family income as can be seen in Table B.5 in Appendix B. Education still adds the most explanation of income immobility (ranging from 21.7 to 27.6 percent), followed by occupation at the age of 30 (with about 14 percent). Considering family income, up to almost 42 percent are explained by the decomposition analysis.

Reiterating, only allowing for education as a pathway of intergenerational transmission, the part of β that is explained by this pathway comprises:

$$\lambda_{Ed1}\gamma_{Ed1} + \lambda_{Ed2}\gamma_{Ed2} + \lambda_{Ed3}\gamma_{Ed3},$$

where each element is estimated using the regression equations (4.8) - (4.11). The results of the regression estimates for the first sequential analysis—the education-only model—is shown in Table 4.6. The first column presents the coefficients of the regression equations (4.8) - (4.10), the second column points out the education coefficients from regression (4.11) displaying earning returns for the levels of educational attainment. The third column summarizes the percentage variation explained by a specific educational level. Nearly all the estimated coefficients are significant.

Table 4.6: Sequential Analysis I - Education Decomposition

Factors	Effect of parental income on factor (λ)	Return to factor (γ)	Percent of total β
Ed1: "at least high school"	0.069** (0.030)	0.191** (0.085)	4.8%
Ed2: "at least some college"	0.220*** (0.042)	−0.163 (0.112)	−13.0%
Ed3: "completed college"	0.195*** (0.041)	0.436*** (0.112)	30.8%
Education total			22.6%

Significance levels: *** < 0.01, ** < 0.05, and * < 0.1.

As the results in Table 4.6 highlight, the influence of family background is weak for high school graduates, but increases for higher levels of educational attainment. Large differences in returns to specific levels of educational attainment are mainly responsible for earnings inequality in the child generation. Especially college graduation yields high returns, substantially causing the great importance of education in the intergenerational transmission. Compared to the next lower level of educational attainment, graduating from college explains 30 percent of total β. This is even more than the percentage explained by total education (amounting to 22 percent), as returns for "at least some college" are negative.

In order to check for robustness of the selected categorization of educational attainment, two further categorical systems are applied. First, years in school and in training are alternatively indicated as a measure of educational achievement.[18] Second, categorical variables are defined according to German educational attainment at the secondary stage. For the alternative categorical systems, the results of the decomposition for the education-only model are shown in Tables B.6 and B.7 in Appendix B, indicating robustness of the results to different measures. For any categorization at lower levels of educational attainment the influence of parental income is weak, but increasing with the achieved educational level. Showing similarities with regard to the return for educational attainment, both a minimum level and high levels of educational

[18]This is standard in the empirical literature measuring educational achievement (for this, see, for example, Blanden (2013)).

achievements are rewarded with high returns; some levels lying in between are marked with negative returns.[19] Taking years in education as categories, the variables nearly explain the same percentage variation in β as with the initial categorization (21.9 percent compared to 22.6 percent).[20]

Table 4.7 shows the detailed decomposition of the third sequential analysis in which all pathway factors are included except for occupational achievements at the age of 34. For education and occupation parental influence is still rather important. But the great importance of both pathway factors in explaining intergenerational immobility is mainly because of high returns for the highest level of education and occupation, respectively. In absolute values, both education and occupation explain even more then the respective estimated shares of total β of about 27 percent and 16 percent, as for both factors some levels of achievement yield negative returns compared to the next lower level. With regard to the occupation categorization, using the European ESeC categorization as occupation measure does not fundamentally change the results as highlighted in Table B.9 in Appendix B.

Comparing the women cohort with the men cohort of the German sample, from descriptive statistics (Table B.1 in Appendix B and Table 4.4, respectively) some variations are ascertained between the two cohorts: in Germany, women tend to be better educated than men. For example, on average four percentage points more women at least graduate from high school. At both the age of 22 and 30 considerably more women are married (11/48.5 percent compared to 5.2/34.7 percent of men). Finally, except for the highest level of occupational achievement, women are on average more represented in each occupation class. For example, 66.4 percent of women at the age of 30 reach the third occupational level "intermediate occupation", at the same age only 46.1 percent of men reach it.

[19]Here, minimum level of educational achievements are at least nine years and at least "Hauptschulabschluss", respectively; high levels include at least 15 years and at least "Allgemeine Hochschulreife", respectively.

[20]The second alternative of measuring educational achievements—German educational attainment at secondary stage—only provides explanation of about 12.5 percent of β but it only incorporates educational levels up to the secondary stage of education and thus considers less educational status at older ages.

Table 4.7: Sequential Analysis III - Decomposition Results

Factors	Effect of parental income on factor (λ)	Return to factor (γ)	Percent of total β
Educational attainment			
*Ed*1	0.069**	0.141*	3.6%
	(0.030)	(0.077)	
*Ed*2	0.220***	−0.119	−9.5%
	(0.042)	(0.104)	
*Ed*3	0.195***	0.470***	33.1%
	(0.041)	(0.108)	
Early Marriage			
Marriage before or at 22	−0.026	0.206*	−1.9%
	(0.019)	(0.121)	
Labor Market Attachment in the 22 to 25 age group			
No work/ training	0.008	−0.361**	−1.1%
	(0.023)	(0.150)	
Full-time position/ training	0.037	0.027	0.4%
	(0.028)	(0.124)	
Marriage and Health at the age of 30			
Married at age 30	−0.004	0.092	−0.1%
	(0.040)	(0.059)	
Excellent Health	0.045	−0.162**	−2.7%
	(0.033)	(0.066)	
Poor (or Fair) Health	−0.003	−0.028	0.0%
	(0.016)	(0.137)	
Labor Market Attachment in the 26 to 29 age group			
No work/ training	−0.011	−0.454***	1.8%
	(0.017)	(0.169)	
Full-time position/ training	0.034	0.326***	4.0%
	(0.029)	(0.113)	
Occupational achievement at the age of 30			
*Occ*1	0.141***	0.066	3.4%
	(0.029)	(0.089)	
*Occ*2	0.206***	−0.129	−9.6%
	(0.039)	(0.131)	
*Occ*3	0.200***	−0.013	−0.9%
	(0.040)	(0.164)	
*Occ*4	0.147***	0.138	7.4%
	(0.041)	(0.143)	
*Occ*5	0.145***	−0.084	−4.4%
	(0.040)	(0.106)	
*Occ*6	0.238***	0.237***	20.5%
	(0.033)	(0.090)	

Significance levels: *** < 0.01, ** < 0.05, and * < 0.1.

When comparing the decomposition results of men and women (Table 4.5 versus Table B.4 in Appendix B) differences become obvious, in particular for the education pathway. For the women cohort education is the sole pathway whose influence is significant, but only for the first two sequential analyses presented in columns (1) and (2) of Table B.4.[21] In the education-only model, for German women almost 60 percent of the income persistence across generations is explained by education and thus nearly two-thirds more than for the comparable men cohort.

Table B.3 in Appendix B represents the regression estimates for German women that lie behind the first sequential analysis (which only includes education). Comparing these results with the findings for men (presented in Table 4.6) shows that two major differences are responsible for differences in the explanatory power of education for men and women in Germany. First, for all educational attainments the influence of family background is much higher for women than for men. Second, for women the return to education is positive, regardless of the level of education. Here the return in achieving the second level of education, "attend college", is highest, accounting for nearly 38 percent of intergenerational income immobility, whereas for men this educational level yields negative return (explaining -13 percent of β).

Intergenerational Transmission in International Comparison

Similarities and differences are illustrated between Germany, Great Britain, and the United States with regard to the importance of potential pathway factors in the intergenerational transmission of income inequality. Note that results from cross-national differences are more robust than those at the country level. Table B.10 in Appendix B shows the descriptive statistics for main variables of the men cohorts in Germany, Great Britain, and the United States.[22] Germany tends to be better educated than Great Britain, but the United States seems to be the most educated of these nations. Compared to the two European countries, in the United States a substantially higher share of men are married both at the age of 22 and 30. In Germany, considerably less people report both

[21] For completeness, besides the influence of education, the estimates of β are highly significant for women.

[22] In the following comparative study, data and results for Great Britain and the United States fall back on the empirical investigation in Blanden et al. (2014).

that their health is excellent and poor or fair compared to both other nations. With regard to labor market attachment Great Britain differs from both other nations, demonstrating the highest participation. In the other nations a similar pattern is seen for labor market attachment in the 22-25 age group, but at the 26-29 age group labor market participation increases more in the United States than in Germany. Finally, compared to the English-speaking countries, in Germany the share of men in the top level of occupational achievement at the age of 30 is highest, but smallest for all other levels of occupation. At the age of 34 the share of men in each occupational level is smallest in Germany. Summing up, the three nations are quite similar, or put differently, none of the countries is substantially different compared to each of the others.

The results of the sequential analyses are presented in Table 4.5 for Germany, Table B.11 for Great Britain and Table B.12 for the United States (the latter both in Appendix B). In international comparison, substantial differences appear in explaining intergenerational transmission of income inequality: with regard to the education-only model, in the United States about 48 percent of total β are explained by education, whereas in Germany and Great Britain the percentage variation which is explained is less than 30 percent (23 percent and 29 percent, respectively). The absolute difference between the United States and the European countries is even larger, as intergenerational income immobility is largest in the United States. Marriage and health status do not have a great influence in intergenerational transmission in any of the three countries as does labor market attachment. Here, the results suggest somewhat more similarity between Great Britain and Germany: when adding early marriage and labor market attachment in the 22-25 age group, the former has a negative effect on β in both European countries and a positive effect in the United States; the opposite is true for the latter. Showing similarities in all the three countries, education and occupation are most relevant in intergenerational transmission, but the explanatory power and the relative weighting of these pathway factors distinguish between the countries. Occupation at the age of 30 explains about 20 percent of β in the three countries—exactly 16.3 percent in Germany, 18 percent in the United States and 21.9 percent in Great Britain. In Great Britain, contrary to both other countries, the share of intergenerational immobility explained by occupation is higher than that explained by education.

Table 4.8 presents an overview of the decomposition results for the sequential analyses in international comparison. Starting from the education-only model, in none of the countries does the aggregated explanatory power of the pathway factors substantially alter when including early marriage and labor market attachment at the 22-25 age group. For both European countries this changes when occupation as a pathway of intergenerational transmission is added to the model: including the child-occupation connection, a total of 43.9 (45.2) percent of β are explained by the pathway factors for Germany (Great Britain) thus being accountable for 17.2 percent (11.4 percent). Unlike Germany and Great Britain, in the United States the occupation pathway only marginally increases the share of income immobility that is in total explained by the pathway factors—from 49.3 percent in sequential analysis II to 52.9 percent in sequential analysis III. Hence, the child-occupation connection does not contribute much to explain income immobility in the United States, but rather seems to absorb explanatory power that had been ascribed to education.[23]

Summarizing, in all three nations education and occupation tend to play major roles in explaining intergenerational income immobility. The explanatory power of education is highest in the United States. When including the child-occupation connection, in Germany and Great Britain the part of β explained by the pathway factors included substantially increases, whereas in the United States the additional explanation of total β is negligible. Including all control variables, in both English-speaking countries about 50 percent of income immobility is explained, in Germany the fraction is about 36 percent. But note that in the case of Germany, variables falling back on observation in the mid-thirties lack quality and validity.

Analyzing reasons that lie behind international similarities and differences, Table 4.9 shows the results of the regression estimates of the education-only model for Germany, Great Britain, and the United States. Generally, parental influence is weaker for lower educational levels. The highest influence is found in the United States. The cross-national differences in parental influence, how-

[23]For more information about the estimates and results for Great Britain and the United States see Blanden et al. (2014).

Table 4.8: Sequential Decomposition - International Comparison

Sequential Analysis I	Part of Total β			Percent of Total β		
	D	GB[a]	USA[a]	D	GB[a]	USA[a]
Missing values	-0.004	0.001	0.000	-1.4%	0.4%	0.1%
Explained component	0.062	0.086	0.185	22.6%	29.3%	48.1%
Unexplained component	0.218	0.207	0.199	78.9%	70.3%	51.8%
Sequential Analysis II	Part of Total β			Percent of Total β		
	D	GB[a]	USA[a]	D	GB[a]	USA[a]
Missing values	-0.005	0.002	-0.003	-1.8%	0.8%	-0.8%
Explained component	0.074	0.100	0.190	26.7%	33.8%	49.3%
Unexplained component	0.207	0.193	0.198	75.1%	65.3%	51.5%
Sequential Analysis III	Part of Total β			Percent of Total β		
	D	GB[a]	USA[a]	D	GB[a]	USA[a]
Missing values	0.017	0.002	0.012	6.0%	0.7%	3.1%
Explained component	0.121	0.133	0.204	43.9%	45.2%	52.9%
Unexplained component	0.138	0.159	0.169	50.1%	54.1%	44.0%
Sequential Analysis IV	Part of Total β			Percent of Total β		
	D	GB[a]	USA[a]	D	GB[a]	USA[a]
Missing values	0.016	0.002	0.016	6.0%	0.8%	4.1%
Explained component	0.102	0.153	0.210	36.8%	51.8%	54.6%
Unexplained component	0.158	0.140	0.159	57.2%	47.4%	41.3%

Significance levels: *** < 0.01, ** < 0.05, and * < 0.1.

[a] Estimates for Great Britain and the United States are taken from Blanden et al. (2014).

Table 4.9: Influence of Education in International Comparison

	Effect of parental income on factor (λ)			Return to factor (γ)			Percentage Variation of Total β		
	D	GB[a]	USA[a]	D	GB[a]	USA[a]	D	GB[a]	USA[a]
*Ed*1	0.069	0.159	0.095	0.191	0.124	0.270	4.8%	6.2%	6.7%
*Ed*2	0.220	0.225	0.304	-0.163	0.099	0.191	-13.0%	7.1%	15.1%
*Ed*3	0.195	0.193	0.239	0.436	0.227	0.424	30.8%	13.9%	26.3%
Education total							22.6%	27.2%	48.1%

Significance levels: *** < 0.01, ** < 0.05, and * < 0.1.
[a] Estimates for Great Britain and the United States are taken from Blanden et al. (2014).

ever, do not primarily explain differences in the explanatory power of education in the transmission process. Actually, varying returns on education are mainly responsible for the differences in the explanatory power of education. The United States generally exhibits relatively high returns on education, despite the highest return on education being realized in Germany for the highest educational attainment level. Achieving this highest educational level separately explains about 30 percent of total β in Germany. Hence, even if Germany and Great Britain at first glance seem more similar than the United States regarding the overall effect of education, individual regression results in Table 4.9 present a different picture. In Great Britain returns on education are quite low compared to both other nations. Unlike Great Britain, in Germany the relatively low percentage variation of β that is in total explained by education is reducible to negative returns at the intermediate level of educational attainment.

Table 4.10 shows single estimation results of the various categories for occupation, at the age of 30 for Germany and at the age of 34 for Great Britain and the United States.[24] As for education, parental influence on occupational achievements does not seem to be the main driving force for international differences, but rather the return on occupational levels. In contrast to education, in all of the three nations return on occupational levels sometimes have neg-

[24] Note that German data regarding occupation at the age of 34 lacks quality and validity since less data is available for men at this age. On these grounds the comparison between Germany and the two english-speaking countries should be handle with care.

Table 4.10: Influence of Occupation in International Comparison

	Effect of parental income on factor (λ)			Return to factor (γ)			Percentage Variation of Total β		
	D	GB[a]	USA[a]	D	GB[a]	USA[a]	D	GB[a]	USA[a]
*Occ*1	0.141	0.121	0.094	0.066	-0.059	-0.114	3.4%	-1.0%	-2.8%
*Occ*2	0.206	0.187	0.191	-0.129	0.158	0.087	-9.6%	6.5%	4.3%
*Occ*3	0.200	0.185	0.209	-0.013	0.015	-0.079	-0.9%	1.1%	-4.3%
*Occ*4	0.147	0.184	0.192	0.138	-0.097	0.190	7.4%	-6.1%	9.5%
*Occ*5	0.145	0.196	0.176	-0.084	0.161	-0.054	-4.4%	10.7%	-2.5%
*Occ*6	0.238	0.136	0.116	0.237	0.176	0.202	20.5%	8.1%	6.1%
Occupation Total							16.4%	19.3%	10.3%

Significance levels: *** < 0.01, ** < 0.05, and * < 0.1.
[a] Estimates for Great Britain and the United States are taken from Blanden et al. (2014).

ative values. Hence, according to the positive amount, the overall effect of occupation is higher in all three nations.

As theory predicts, returns on educational attainment play a major role in the intergenerational transmission process and thus the prevailing intergenerational income immobility in society. Therefore the effect of the internationally different return on education is quantified showing the importance of these returns. Using the education-only model, the intergenerational income elasticity is calculated and also the explanatory power of education for the hypothetical case that respective British or American returns on education would apply in Germany. Formally, the calculation is based on the following decomposition of β:

$$\beta = \lambda_{Ed1,D}\gamma_{Ed1,j} + \lambda_{Ed2,D}\gamma_{Ed2,j} + \lambda_{Ed3,D}\gamma_{Ed3,j} + \gamma_{inc,D},$$

where j marks the respective country, Great Britain and the United States. Parental influence is taken into account as existing in Germany (thus marked with D).

Table 4.11 presents the results of these hypothetical considerations. The situation would not change fundamentally if Germany would have the same returns as those existing in Great Britain. The explanatory power of educa-

Table 4.11: Effect of Varying Return on Education within Germany

	Hypothetical considerations		
	with German Returns	with GB Returns[a]	with US Returns[a]
Total β^b	0.276	0.288	0.357
Part of β explained by education	0.062	0.075	0.143
Percent of β explained by education	22.6%	25.9%	40.1%

Significance levels: *** < 0.01, ** < 0.05, and * < 0.1.
[a] Estimates for Great Britain and the United States are taken from Blanden et al. (2014).
[b] For calculating total β the estimates of the missing values and the unexplained component in the case of Germany are taken into account.

tion would only be higher by 3.3 percentage points. Applying the returns on education that exist in the United States, intergenerational income elasticity would reach about 0.36 and thus would be much higher than is actually the case in Germany. In this case education would be responsible for 40 percent of the intergenerational immobility.

4.3 Implications

Up to 40 percent of the intergenerational income elasticity that exists in Germany is explained by the pathway factors education, occupation, labor market attachment, marital status, and health status. Primarily the former two are the main forces in transmitting economic advantage and disadvantage across generations. Accounting for at least 20 percent of the intergenerational income immobility, education is the most important channel in the intergenerational transmission process in Germany.

Similarities are shown between Germany, Great Britain, and the United States: in all three nations education and occupation are the main channels through which economic advantage and disadvantage are passed. However, compared to the two European countries, the explanatory power of education in the intergenerational transmission is substantially higher in the United States. This explains nearly 50 percent of the intergenerational income immobility (compared to less than 30 percent in both other countries). The most likely explanation for this result is the comparatively high return on education in the United States. Reasons for the differences between the United States and the European countries vary for Germany and Great Britain: in contrast to the United States, in Great Britain occupation is the main driving force for intergenerational transmission of income inequality. In Germany, however, education is the main pathway of intergenerational transmission and at least in part substantial returns on education can be achieved. The highest return on education, for example, is realized in Germany when men attain the highest educational level. Still, there is a gap between the explanatory power of education in Germany and the United States because of negative returns for intermediate educational levels in Germany. Summarizing, despite varying reasons, international differences in the return on education (occupation) are primarily responsible for the importance of education (occupation) as a pathway of intergenerational transmission and thus the degree of intergenerational income immobility within a country.

The relatively low explanatory power of education as a pathway of intergenerational transmission in Germany causes a jump to the conclusion that this pathway plays a less important role in Germany than in the United States. In absolute values, however, the explanatory power of education is similar in both countries. Attaining the highest educational level actually explains about 30 percent of the intergenerational immobility that exists in Germany. The negative returns for intermediate educational level are puzzling, particularly in consideration of the fact that these are robust to a different categorization of educational attainment. Therefore further research is necessary to investigate reasons for this pattern.

In Germany education as a pathway of intergenerational transmission of income inequality is relatively more important for women than for men. This explains an additional two-thirds of the intergenerational income elasticity, whereas the elasticities are nearly the same. Varying influence of family background and varying returns on education are responsible for these gender differences. First, family background is substantially more significant for women than for men. Second, in contrast to men, women realize positive, and relatively high, returns when attaining the intermediate educational level, but relatively small returns when achieving the highest educational level. The small return on education for the highest level of education is in part accountable for gender differences in earnings. Although the percentage of women who attain the highest educational level is approximately the same as the percentage of men, women are under-represented in the highest occupational positions.

Public policy such as female quotas in leading positions would enhance the percentage of women in high occupational position and thus their earnings. Assuming that the highest educational level is required for these occupational positions, such public policy would also increase the return on this educational level. Whether intergenerational income mobility thus decreases depends on the effect of such a policy on the return on the intermediate level of education. If the return on the intermediate educational level is unaffected, intergenerational income mobility decreases with the implementation of female quotas in leading positions. However, whether or not intergenerational income mobility decreases, such policy may bridge the gender gap.

Whether and how public policy may counteract existing gender differences concerning the importance of family background are open questions. Answers to these questions necessitates further research. In any case, public policies that provide higher education or lower barriers for these kinds of education diminishes the influence of family background and thus unambiguously increases intergenerational income mobility.

Chapter 5

Conclusions

This part focuses on how education investment influences intergenerational income mobility both on theoretical and empirical grounds. As demonstrated in the theory-based study in Chapter 3, public education does not unambiguously increase intergenerational income mobility. The interactive effect of public education and private human capital investment accounts for the impact of education policy on income mobility. Education policy will increase intergenerational income mobility only if public and private human capital investment are substitutes for each other. If public education crowds-in private human capital investment or does not affect it, the implementation of such policy measures will even decrease income mobility.

The study illustrates the importance of human capital accumulation. Besides a child's abilities, his or her human capital received—and thus personal economic success—depends on family background. Private human capital investment increases with the productivity of human capital investment and the earnings return on human capital. The same holds true for the differences in these investments due to varying family background. As a result, intergenerational income mobility is lower, the more productive human capital investment, the higher the earnings return on human capital, and the greater the influence of parental income.

Both family background and the return on human capital investment mainly influence a child's level of received human capital investment thus determining the strength of the economic parent-child connection. Capturing this causality, the influence of potential pathway factors, such as education, on the economic parent-child linkage in Germany was empirically estimated. Accounting for 20 percent of the intergenerational income immobility in Germany, education is the most important channel through which economic advantage and disadvantage are passed across generations. Education and occupation together are accountable for 40 percent of the existing immobility.

Showing similarities between Germany, Great Britain, and the United States,[1] education and occupation are the main channels of intergenerational transmission in all three countries. However, the degree of immobility and the explanatory power of both factors influencing the immobility differ across the countries. It turns out that varying returns on the respective pathway are mainly responsible for the international differences. Here as theory predicts, higher returns on education yield a high income persistence across generations, with education being predominately accountable for this persistence. Realizing the highest return on education on average, the United States is less mobile than both European countries. In addition, in the United States education explains nearly 50 percent of the existing immobility, whereas in Germany and Great Britain the explanatory power of education is less than 30 percent.

Not all redistributive policy measures that reduce economic inequality enhance intergenerational income mobility. If policy measures either reduce parental influence or decrease the earning return on human capital investment, the parent-child connection will decline, and thus increase mobility. In this context, education policy will increase intergenerational mobility only if public education crowds out private human capital investment, thus lowering the importance of family background.

Most likely policy measures intending to increase intergenerational income mobility aim at lowering parental influence, rather than reducing the return on human capital investment. However, the empirical research in Chapter 4 indicates that while family background plays an important role, varying returns on education and occupation, respectively, are accountable for the better part of international differences in the mobility level. If, for example, the German returns on education would be equal to those prevalent in the United States, intergenerational income immobility would be much higher—amounting to 0.36 rather than 0.28. Thus, if public policy tries to tackle immobility, measures decreasing the return on education would be most effective. Whether such a decrease is desirable from an allocative perspective is a completely different matter.

[1] Here, the results of Great Britain and the United States are taken from Blanden et al. (2014).

According to Becker and Tomes (1986), the functioning of the capital market crucially influences the degree of mobility within a country. A less smoothly functioning capital market lowers income mobility, as it increases parental influences on the child's achievements, for example in education. Hence by decreasing the importance of family background a governmental measure will increase mobility if it guarantees smooth implementation of the capital market. This is all the more true for the United States, where tertiary education is mainly financed privately. Thus, in contrast to Germany, in the United States policies aimed at increasing intergenerational income mobility should focus on granting all citizens access to capital markets. Otherwise, compared to Germany, in the United States income would be even more immobile across generations.

Part II

Social Beliefs about Income Mobility and the Demand for Redistribution

Chapter 6

Introduction

At present, the refusal of extensive redistributive policy in the U.S. population is conspicuous when tracing Obama's attempt to reform the health care system. In contrast to the United States, there is much less opposition to redistributive policies in Germany, and the formation of a political movement like the tea party is not in sight. Regarding lump-sum transfer payments financed by proportional income taxation, such a redistributive measure is theoretically beneficial for all individuals with below-average incomes. Hence, as income distribution is generally skewed to the right, economic theory predicts the support for redistributive policy to increase with income inequality.[1] All the more surprising, the United States is more averse to redistribution, although income inequality in the United States is higher than in Germany. Consequently, factors other than the relative position in the income distribution must additionally influence individual preferences for redistribution. These factors are addressed in the literature, such as in Alesina and Glaeser (2004) who compare the size of the welfare state between continental European countries and the United States. According to Alesina and Glaeser, varieties in social beliefs, political institutions, and/or social heterogeneity are the main reasons for international differences.

Concentrating on social beliefs about the determinants of personal economic success, Part II of this thesis addresses how these beliefs influence society in the long run. Here I reveal the consequences of both real and perceived economic conditions within society on (i) the incentives to work, (ii) the demand for redistribution, and finally, (iii) the intergenerational income mobility within society. Understanding the causality of social beliefs regarding the determinants of personal economic success and redistributive policy measures more deeply, enables the government to better act and react when aiming to promote greater equality of opportunity and/or increase income mobility.

[1] For more information, see Meltzer and Richard (1981).

It is conceivable that although the individuals of society know the determinants of income, they do not know the relative importance of these determinants. Thus, with uncertainty about the main determinants, individuals form beliefs regarding the importance of effort and family background for personal economic success. Depending on individual experiences of intergenerational income mobility, different beliefs about the composition of income arise. Here experiencing upward mobility strengthens the beliefs that put more weight on effort rather than predetermined factors. Hence, individuals that experience upward mobility believe more strongly in self-determined rather than exogenously determined factors. As these individuals regard the income distribution to be quite just, they are more averse to redistribution. In this context Piketty (1995) shows that individual preferences for redistribution may differ because of varying individual beliefs, even if the distributive aim is equal across society and there is *a priori* no social conflict.[2]

Not only the real chance of social advancement, but also the perceived chance, crucially influences society, its demand for redistribution, and its members' willingness to invest in personal effort. How both the real role and the socially believed role of effort as crucial for economic success influence effort, the level of redistribution, and the income distribution in society is initially investigated in Chapter 8.

Here despite abstracting from conflicting views about social objectives within society, I take account of the fact that social value judgments may vary across countries. In addition, assuming that societies may be more or less dynastically altruistic, I analyze how the size of dynastic altruism influences society. It turns out that dynastic altruism enhances individual willingness to invest in effort. When opportunities are not equal across individuals, parents take into account the positive effect of being successful on their children's prospects of success. Therefore, compared to completely selfish societies, in dynastically altruistic societies its members are more aware of prevalent inequality of opportunity. Thus, dynastic altruism strengthens preferences for redistribution.

Individual beliefs regarding the role of effort significantly influence incentives to work and the demand for redistribution. The more weight an individual puts

[2]Piketty (1995) indicates the influence of varying beliefs about the determinants of personal economic success on the voting pattern in society.

on hard work as the crucial factor, the more he or she is willing to invest in effort, and the less redistribution he or she prefers. However, at the aggregate level, it turns out that the effect of changes in social beliefs is ambiguous rather than straightforward and critically depends on social value judgments. Only if society is sufficiently concerned about its least well-off members, will changes in social beliefs putting more weight on the role of effort set additional incentives to invest in effort and will decrease the demand for redistribution in society. Contrarily, a marginal increase in the real role of effort—that is, the real marginal rate of return on effort—unambiguously increases redistribution in society. Thus, although one unit of effort is actually more valuable, effort decreases due to tax incentives.[3]

Exogenously determined factors such as family background critically influence a child's prospects of success. The greater the inequality of opportunity due to varying social origins, the more disadvantageous it is to be born into a poor family. Thus, the success of society in offering equal opportunities not only affects income mobility in society, but also the demand for redistribution. Hence, the prevalent inequality of opportunity affects society through various channels. In fact, the impact of a reduction of inequality of opportunity on incentives to work turns out to be ambiguous. They depend on social beliefs about the role of effort, the degree of dynastic altruism, and social value judgments. If a society underestimates the role of effort,[4] greater equality of opportunity will always increase the willingness to work. Thus, prospects of social advancement are enhanced with increasing effort. However, if society overestimates the role of effort, in societies with pronounced dynastic altruism for example, greater equality of opportunity will decrease individual effort. In this case, the chance of social advancement will also decrease.

In addition to inequality of opportunity, incentives to work crucially influence intergenerational income mobility. Whether policy measures that reduce inequality of opportunity also increases income mobility in society is critically linked to social beliefs regarding the role of effort. As it turns out, only if

[3]Note that with uncertainty regarding the role of effort, when the real role of effort changes, members of society notice changing prospects of success without knowing where this comes from.

[4]Here underestimating (overestimating) the role of effort means that the socially believed role is lower (higher) than the real role of effort weighted by inequality of opportunity.

society puts insufficient weight on effort, will policy measures providing more equality of opportunity simultaneously increase intergenerational income mobility. In addition, the degree of dynastic altruism reduces the likelihood that intergenerational income mobility increases with greater equality of opportunity.

Part II is organized as follows: Chapter 7 illustrates the related literature on the topic. Chapter 8 first addresses on a theoretical level how social beliefs influence society in the long-run, the incentives to work, and the demand for redistribution. Then, the efficacy of policy measures that reduce inequality of opportunity in increasing income mobility is analyzed. Chapter 9 reviews empirical evidence of the importance of social beliefs for the support of redistributive policy. Finally, Chapter 10 summarizes Part II.

Chapter 7

Related Literature

There is a growing consensus in economic literature that culture, as revealing social norms, values, and beliefs, crucially influences society and potentially produces critical economic consequences. Thus, to understand its causality on the microeconomic level is of great significance, as it enables us to address the source of the deficiency. Social norms and beliefs may affect both the willingness to cooperate in society and the effectiveness of political institutions. For example, social beliefs regarding equality of opportunity determine the perception of equity in income distribution. Regarding social beliefs, there are mainly two strands of literature. On the one hand, the literature focuses on how individual beliefs are formed and transmitted over time. On the other hand, economic research addresses how these individual beliefs interact with the economic and institutional environment.[1] The theory-based study in Chapter 8 is associated with the former strand of literature. Here the focus is on social beliefs regarding the determinants of personal economic success and investigates its impact on incentives to work, the demand for redistribution, and finally, income mobility.

Focusing on redistribution, Meltzer and Richard (1981) demonstrate that an individual's position in the income distribution in society determines his or her preferences for redistribution.[2] Here they consider lump-sum transfer payments financed by proportional income taxation. Thus, individuals with below-average income benefit from such redistributive measures. As Meltzer and Richard show, when voting on income tax rates and thus redistribution, the voter with median income is the decisive voter. As income distribution is generally skewed to the right, implying that median income is smaller than average income, the majority of society favors such measures of redistribution.

[1] An example for this is the contribution of Tabellini (2008).

[2] Also the studies of Romer (1975) and Roberts (1977) address the idea that the relative position in the income distribution in society influences individual preferences for redistribution.

In addition, the level of redistribution increases with pre-tax income inequality. There is consensus in the economic literature that the individual position in the income distribution is important. However, recent research give rise to doubts that this is the single determinant of individual preferences for redistribution. Hence, a growing body of literature address individual preferences for redistribution.[3]

The hypothesis stated by Meltzer and Richard (1981) requires that individuals be able to react immediately when it comes to changes in their relative income position. Thus, this implies that elections are held continuously which is not actually the case. Hence, when voting on redistribution, individuals take into account both their current and their future income. In this context, Benabou and Ok (2001) formally examine the idea that if redistributive policies are long-lasting, prospects of upward mobility will influence current preferences for redistribution. These prospects of upward mobility induce individuals to oppose high levels of redistribution, although they will currently benefit from such redistributive policies. Hence, even though more than fifty percent of society is poorer than average in terms of current income, a majority rationally votes against redistribution on a large scale.[4]

In contrast to Benabou and Ok (2001), Piketty (1995) considers experiences of past income mobility rather than expectations of future income mobility.[5] Piketty (1995) shows that individual preferences towards redistributive politics may differ across society, although *a priori* the distributive aim is equal within society. Here varying individual preferences result from different beliefs regarding the determinants of personal economic success. With uncertainty regarding the relative importance of these determinants, past income history affects individual beliefs about what drives economic success. Thus, associated with the literature on belief formation, experiences of intergenerational income mobility influence individual beliefs regarding income determinants. As a consequence,

[3]In this context Alesina and Giuliano (2011) provide a review of the determinants of individual preferences for redistribution. In addition, they include empirical evidence of the hypothesis stated mostly for the United States, but also cross-national comparisons.

[4]In addition, Benabou and Ok (2001) empirically estimate the effect of prospective upward mobility drawing back on U.S. data. According to their study, the effect mentioned exists, but likely is dominated by social insurance aspects.

[5]Both of these causalities—concerning experiences and expectation of income mobility—were originally stated by Hirschman and Rothschild (1973); the former being referred to as the "tunnel effect".

if an individual believes that hard work matters more than other factors, he or she significantly invests in effort, but prefer relatively low levels of redistribution. Hence, according to Piketty (1995), left-wing voters who strongly support redistributive policies are more represented in low-income classes than in high-income classes. In addition, left-wing voters are more represented in low-income classes than right-wing voters who are more averse to redistributive policies.

Building up on the Piketty-framework, in Chapter 8 I go one step further by analyzing how real and perceived economic conditions critically influence incentives to work and the support for redistributive policies in the long-run. It turns out that the real and average believed roles of effort have completely different effects on society. Mostly, social beliefs putting significant weight on effort as the crucial factor increase effort, but lower the level of redistributive policies, while the opposite holds true for the real role of effort. In contrast to Piketty (1995), I additionally take into account varying social objectives and the possibility of dynastic altruism. As it results, both varying social objectives and the degree of dynastic altruism affect not only incentives to work and the demand for redistribution, but also the impact of policy measures promoting greater equality of opportunity on income mobility.

Comparing Germany and the United States, Germany exhibits less income inequality and tends to be a more mobile society. Hence, according to both the Meltzer-Richard model and the effect of prospective upward mobility, the support for and thus the level of redistribution should be higher in the United States. Actually this is not the case. In this regard, rather than rationally held expectations of future upward mobility, over-optimism about future prospects of social advancement can be a reason for expecting to increase one's income. In this context, Benabou and Tirole (2006) establish a theory of collective beliefs resulting from "indoctrination". Based on the model of Piketty (1995), they investigate how the need to believe in a just world where everyone gets what they deserve evolves and how it affects society. As they show, what actually matters is not whether social beliefs[6] conform with reality, but whether they are more optimistic and less pessimistic. If collective beliefs within society are more optimistic, the support for redistribution will be relatively low and

[6] Here social beliefs are seen as endogenously shared ideology.

incentives to work relatively high. In the long run, such societies are characterized by large income inequality and low levels of redistribution. Otherwise, being more pessimistic, societies exhibit low inequality, but an extensive welfare state. Hence, as demonstrated by Benabou and Tirole, different collective beliefs across countries are successful in explaining international differences in political ideology and the level of redistribution.[7]

Focusing on the desire for fairness, Alesina and Angeletos (2005) examine how the source of income inequality influences the demand for redistribution. Thus, the level of redistribution resulting from the political process depends on social beliefs about how fair social competition is and what determines income inequality. If the members of society are highly motivated to work, they will vote against an extensive welfare state. In such societies, although income inequality is high, the demand for redistribution is relatively low because income tends to be fairly distributed in large part. By contrast, in societies with a rather low willingness to work, although income inequality is low, society favors high levels of redistribution, as income distribution is seen to be highly unfair.

In recent decades, the question as to what drives the demand for redistribution has attracted attention in the field of economics. Capturing the importance of social beliefs, the study in Chapter 8 shows that both real and socially perceived economic conditions significantly influence society in the long run. In contrast to the existing literature, how social beliefs regarding the role of effort affect the aim of increasing intergenerational income mobility is additionally investigated. It turns out that whether policy measures promoting greater equality of opportunity also increase intergenerational income mobility significantly depends on social beliefs regarding hard work as crucial for economic success.

[7] In line with this, Benabou (2000) deals with the issue of how countries with equal initial economic and political condition differ so greatly with regard to redistribution. In his study, due to more political power and coordination in high-income classes, he supposes the decisive voter to be an agent with income higher than median income. Assuming imperfect capital and insurance markets, he shows that countries may end up in completely different steady states: on the one hand, countries may feature a low level of redistribution and high income inequality; on the other hand, countries may exhibit low inequality and a high level of redistribution.

Chapter 8

Social Beliefs and Redistributive Politics

With uncertainty about the relative weighting of the income determinants, different beliefs regarding, for example, the role of effort significantly affect incentives to work, the demand for redistribution, and the income distribution in society. These individual beliefs emerge from personal experiences of intergenerational income mobility.

The aim of this chapter is to study (i) how the real and socially believed economic conditions influence long-term equilibrium in society and (ii) whether policy measures that reduce inequality of opportunity also increase intergenerational income mobility. For this purpose, this chapter exhibits a model enabling us to investigate the link between social beliefs and redistributive politics.[1] Regarding cross-national differences, the study takes into account that societies may differ in their degree of dynastic altruism and their social value judgments.

8.1 Incentives to Work and the Demand for Redistribution

Individuals know that both predetermined factors and effort to some extent are important for personal economic success, but not the relative weighting of these factors. Assuming uncertainty about the crucial factor for personal economic success, in this section incentives to work and the demand for redistribution are determined. For this purpose, in section 8.1.1 initially the optimal effort level and the individually preferred tax rate are illustrated assuming the society knows the income determinants with certainty.

---

[1] This model is an extended version of the model in Piketty (1995), including the possibility of dynastic altruism and varying social value judgments. In contrast to Piketty (1995), this study goes one step further investigating the impact of social beliefs on society in the long run including the effect on income mobility.

8.1.1 Optimal Decision under Certainty

A non-overlapping generations model is considered with a discrete and infinite time horizon ($t = 1, 2, ...$). Each time period t can be seen as one generation. In each generation t, society consists of a continuum of agents $i \in [0; 1]$. Assuming that each agent in each generation has exactly one offspring, the general public is constant over time. Below, index t marks the generation considered and index i a representative family dynasty.

Individual life-time income is either high (y_H) or low (y_L) with:

$$\Delta y = y_H - y_L > 0.$$

In the following, life-time income is referred to as income. In generation t, the share of agents born into low-income families (high-income families) is denoted by L_t (H_t). For all generations, the sum of children born into low-income families and those born into high-income families is one, that is:

$$L_t + H_t = 1 \quad \forall t \in T.$$

Whether receiving high income or not depends on an agent's social origins, individual effort, and luck. An agent born into a low-income family receives income y_H with probability:

$$\rho_L := \rho_L(y_{it} = y_{H,t} | e_{it} = e, y_{it-1} = y_L) = \pi_L + \theta\, e \tag{8.1}$$

with $\rho_L < 1$. Analogously, the probability of success for agents born into a high-income family is:

$$\rho_H := \rho_H(y_{it} = y_{H,t} | e_{it} = e, y_{it-1} = y_H) = \pi_H + \theta\, e \tag{8.2}$$

with $\rho_H < 1$. In both cases (8.1) and (8.2), the first term describes the influence of the predetermined factor on personal economic success. For $\pi_L \neq \pi_H$, prospects of success vary with parents' income level. Assuming that $\pi_H > \pi_L$, the probability of success is greater for children born into high-income families than for children born into low-income families. Here $\Delta\pi \equiv \pi_H - \pi_L$ states the extent of inequality of opportunity. The second term, θe, identifies the influence of effort on personal economic success, where e marks the effort level and θ the marginal rate of return on individual effort. The more effort one invests, the more likely he or she achieves y_H. When to invest in effort costs accrue according to the following quadratic cost function:

$$C(e) = \frac{e^2}{2a} \tag{8.3}$$

with the weighting parameter a. The higher a, the less is the arising cost of one unit of effort. When deciding on the individual effort level, agents balance out benefits and costs of a additional marginal unit of effort.

Redistribution takes place by lump-sum transfer payments which are financed by proportional income taxation. Here, $\tau \in [0,1]$ indicates the tax rate and $\tau_t Y_t$ the transfer payment with

$$Y_t = y_L + H_t \Delta y$$

the mean income of generation t.

Assuming dynastic altruism, individuals care about both their own economic situation and the economic situation of their child. Parents are interested in their levels of consumption—indicated by their available income—and the expected income of their child. When deciding on individual effort, the state of affairs of the next generation is unknown and thus, reducing uncertainty, parents focus on the expected social status of their children—stated by the expected gross income.[2] Hence, assuming dynastic altruism, the utility function U_{it} of dynasty i in generation t consists of the available income in t and the expected gross income of the next generation $t+1$ and is:

$$U_{it} = (1-\tau_t)y_{it} + \tau_t Y_t - C(e_{it}) + \gamma E y_{it+1}. \tag{8.4}$$

The first three terms determine the net income in generation t comprising the after-tax income, lump-sum transfer payments, and negatively the accruing cost of effort. The fourth term contains expected gross income of the next generation. Here the parameter $\gamma \in [0,1]$ indicates the degree of dynastic

[2]This is additionally justified by the fact that the effort decision of the child is unknown at the time of parental decision making, as will be shown later.

altruism, measuring the extent generation t takes into account the concerns of generation $t+1$.

In addition to the personal financial situation of the family dynasty, an individual cares about social welfare or more precisely, future social welfare providing the children of the society at least a minimum of equality of opportunity. Abstracting from conflicting views about social objectives, all members of society share the same social value judgments and thus a single social welfare function. Considering social welfare of the children belonging to generation t, the social welfare function is described by:

$$V_t = (1-\delta)EU_{it}\Big|_{y_{it-1}=y_L} + \delta EU_{it}\Big|_{y_{it-1}=y_H} . \tag{8.5}$$

where the parameter $\delta \in [0,1)$ indicates the degree the wealth of agents born into high-income families is considered in the social welfare function. Accordingly, $1-\delta$ indicates the share the wealth of agents born into low-income families is taken into account. Taking at least to a degree the concerns of the least well-off into account is advantageous even for the rich members of society, since a certain standard of living reduces crime. In addition, it enables the members of society at least a minimum level of educational attainment. Hence, in any case it is assumed that $1-\delta > 0$ or put differently, $\delta < 1$. For $\delta = 0$, the welfare function comprises solely the economic situation of the least well-off agents who were born into low-income families. This implies a Rawlsian social welfare function. For $0 < \delta < 1$, the social welfare function considers agents with both social origins. Here the higher the magnitude of δ, the more the needs of agents born into high-income families are taken into account relative to the needs of those born into low-income families. For $\delta = \frac{1}{2}$, the social welfare function is utilitaristic.

In generation t, the time structure is as follows: first, given the tax rate τ_t, generation t decides how much effort it is willing to invest. Then income is realized. Last, the general public votes on the tax rate for the next generation τ_{t+1}.

Optimal Level of Individual Effort

When deciding about the individual effort, agents know the tax rate they are faced with, but not their income level. Based on expectation about future income, the maximization problem differs for agents with varying social origins because of different prospects of economic success. Agents born into low-income families choose the effort level e_{Lt} by solving:[3]

$$e_{Lt}(\tau_t) \in \operatorname{argmax}_{e_{Lt} \geq 0} EU_{it} \Big|_{y_{it-1}=y_L} \tag{8.6}$$

with

$$\begin{aligned} EU_{it} \Big|_{y_{it-1}=y_L} &= (1-\tau_t) E y_{it} \Big|_{y_{it-1}=y_L} + \tau_t Y_t - C(e_{it}) + \gamma E y_{it+1} \Big|_{y_{it-1}=y_L} \\ &= (1-\tau_t)((\pi_L + \theta e_{Lt})\Delta y + y_L) + \tau_t Y_t - \frac{1}{2a} e_{Lt}^2 \\ &\quad + \gamma((\pi_L + \theta e_{Lt})(\rho_{Ht+1} - \rho_{Lt+1})\Delta y + \rho_{Lt+1}\Delta y + y_L). \end{aligned}$$

Analogously, agents born into high-income families choose e_{Ht} by solving:

$$e_{Ht}(\tau_t) \in \operatorname{argmax}_{e_{Ht} \geq 0} EU_{it} \Big|_{y_{it-1}=y_H} \tag{8.7}$$

with

$$\begin{aligned} EU_{it} \Big|_{y_{it-1}=y_H} &= (1-\tau_t) E y_{it} \Big|_{y_{it-1}=y_H} + \tau_t Y_t - C(e_{it}) + \gamma E y_{it+1} \Big|_{y_{it-1}=y_H} \\ &= (1-\tau_t)((\pi_L + \Delta\pi + \theta e_{Ht})\Delta y + y_L) + \tau_t Y_t - \frac{1}{2a} e_{Ht}^2 \\ &\quad + \gamma((\pi_L + \Delta\pi + \theta e_{Ht})(\rho_{Ht+1} - \rho_{Lt+1})\Delta y + \rho_{Lt+1}\Delta y + y_L). \end{aligned}$$

According to the first order conditions[4] of the maximization problems (8.6) and (8.7), the optimal level of effort is given by:

$$e_t = e_{Lt} = e_{Ht} = a\theta\Delta y(1 - \tau_t + \gamma(\rho_{Ht+1} - \rho_{Lt+1})), \tag{8.8}$$

[3] For both type of agents, those born into low-income families and those born into high-income families, the expected utility is derived in Appendix C.1.

[4] The second order conditions are fulfilled so that the resultant level of individual effort maximizes individual utility.

and thus, is independent of social origins. Hence, except for the scale of inequality of opportunity $\Delta\pi$, the probability of success is the same for children born into high-income families and children born into low-income families. This result holds for all generations implying that $\rho_{Ht} - \rho_{Lt} = \Delta\pi$ $(\forall t = 1, 2, ...)$ and thus Equation (8.8) turns into:

$$e_t = (1 - \tau_t)\theta a \Delta y + \gamma \Delta\pi \theta a \Delta y. \tag{8.9}$$

The first term reflects the part of effort that is sensitive to the given tax rate. An increase in the tax rate would lower the incentives to work and thus the effort level. The second term presents the effect of dynastic altruism ($\gamma > 0$): being successful enhances the child's future prospects of success by ensuring him or her the greatest possible opportunities. Hence, when deciding about individual effort, parents are aware of inequality of opportunity their child may be faced with. Thus, the optimal level of effort increases with the extent of inequality of opportunity. Here the scale of dynastic altruism (the size of γ) determines the strength of this effect. An increase in the weighting parameters θ, Δy and a enhances individual effort: the more individual effort pays off (the higher θ), the more one is willing to invest in effort. An increase in the possible loss that agents will suffer if they do not succeed (higher Δy) incentivizes to work. Thus, the higher the expected income disparity is, the more agents are willing to invest in effort. Last, individual effort increases with a, as the costs of effort decline.

Optimal Tax Rate

Generation $t-1$ votes on the tax rate generation t is faced with. At the time of voting, agents know their income level and thus their child's family background, but not the child's achieved income level. Hence, the vote takes place behind the veil of ignorance. When voting on τ_t, generation $t-1$ takes into account the effort decision of generation t:

$$e_t = (1 - \tau_t)\theta a \Delta y + \gamma \Delta\pi \theta a \Delta y$$

as well as the expected average income in generation t:

$$\begin{aligned} EY_t &= L_t(y_L + \rho_{Lt}\Delta y) + H_t(y_L + \rho_{Ht}\Delta y) \\ &= y_L + (\pi_L + \theta e_t)\Delta y + H_t\Delta\pi\Delta y. \end{aligned}$$

Note that H_t (L_t) describes the share of children born into high-income families (low-income families) which is known at the time of vote. Regarding the social welfare function (8.5), the maximization problem is as follows:[5]

$$\tau_t(\Delta\pi, \theta) \in \text{argmax}_{\tau_{it}} V_t \tag{8.10}$$

with

$$\begin{aligned} V_t = {} & y_L(1+\gamma) + \pi_L\Delta y(1+\gamma(1+\Delta\pi)) + \tau H_t\Delta\pi\Delta y + \gamma\theta e_{t+1}\Delta y \\ & + (1-\tau_t+\gamma\Delta\pi)[\frac{1}{2}a\theta^2\Delta y^2(1+\tau_t+\gamma\Delta\pi) + \delta\Delta y\Delta\pi]. \end{aligned}$$

According to the first order condition[6], the tax rate τ_{it} is determined by:

$$\tau_t = \tau_{it} = \frac{(H_t - \delta)\Delta\pi}{\Delta y\theta^2 a} \quad \forall i \in I. \tag{8.11}$$

Independent of social origins, all individuals within society prefer the same tax rate and thus, regarding redistribution, no conflict of interest exists.[7] Political attitudes towards redistribution do not vary with income, but with the underlying social value judgment. As the social objective is the same within society, independent of social origins, each individual prefers the same tax rate τ_t. This tax rate can thus be seen as the socially optimal one denoted by τ_t^{opt}.

The tax rate τ_t increases with the share of agents born into high-income families (H_t), as redistribution becomes more effective. The same pattern is true for $\Delta\pi$: the greater the inequality of opportunity is, the more need to correct it and thus, the higher the tax rate. An increase in θ, however, reduces

[5]The derivation of V_t is presented in Appendix C.2.

[6]The second order condition is fulfilled so that the resultant tax rate maximizes social welfare.

[7]This confirms the results of Piketty (1995) for varying social value judgments. In addition, this highlights that the degree of dynastic altruism does not change the preferences for redistribution.

the tax rate. The larger the income elasticity θ with regard to effort is, the more serious is the moral hazard incentive problem. Different social value judgments across countries affect their demand for redistribution and thus the chosen tax rate as expected: the tax rate is highest under a Rawlsian social welfare function. Taking additionally into account the needs of children born into high-income families ($\delta > 0$) lowers the tax rate. Hence, the more the needs of the well-off are taken into account in society (the higher δ), the less is the demand for redistribution and thus, the lower is the tax rate. Low tax rates provide high incentives to work, since the people who do not achieve high levels of income receive little protection in the form of redistributions of income. In order to avoid negative tax rates, the value range of δ is bounded above with $\delta \leq H_t$ ($\forall t = 0, 1, 2, ...$). Hence, $\delta = H_t$ is the maximal acceptable share to which the needs of children born into high-income families are taken into account in the social welfare function. Otherwise, a society would accept a social welfare function with more weight on the needs of children born into high-income families than the proportion of those children in society. On the upper bound, the tax rate is restricted to one.[8]

Dynastic altruism does not affect the socially optimal tax rate, but rather the willingness to invest in effort. In a completely selfish society ($\gamma = 0$), inequality of opportunity only indirectly influences the individual effort level. Greater inequality of opportunity enhances the demand for redistribution, the tax rate increases, and thus, effort decreases. If a society is dynastically altruistic, individual effort will also be directly affected by $\Delta\pi$. The existing inequality of opportunity in society incentivizes individuals to invest in effort, as the achieved income level determines the child's opportunity and thus, probability of success. The more disadvantageous it is to be born into low-income families, the more parents are willing to invest in effort. Here higher effort levels enhance the chance of being successful and thus ensure the child largest possible starting conditions to be successful as well. Regarding the aggregate effect of inequality of opportunity on effort, for possible parameter values, the indirect negative effect via the tax rate dominates the positive direct effect (as can be seen in Appendix C.3). Hence, greater equality of opportunity unambiguously increases individual effort.

[8]As follows from $\tau_t \leq 1$, $H_t - \delta$ has to be equal or smaller than $\frac{\Delta y \theta^2 a}{\Delta\pi}$ ($\forall t = 0, 1, 2, ...$).

8.1.2 Optimal Decision under Uncertainty: Dynastic Learning

With certainty about the income determinants, all members in society choose the same effort level and the same tax rate independent of social origins. Assuming uncertainty about the main determinants of personal economic success and thus about the true set of parameters (θ^*, π_L^*, $\Delta\pi^*$), family dynasties form beliefs about the weighting of these determinants. These individual beliefs arise from income mobility experiences. Thus although the members of society agree that both effort and predetermined factors are important for personal economic success, they may disagree about the relative quantitative importance of these factors. Hence, unanimity about the individually most preferred tax rate does not have to exist anymore.

Dynastic Learning

Starting with initial beliefs[9] about the set of parameters (θ, π_L, $\Delta\pi$), these beliefs may change over time, as dynasties learn from their experiences of income mobility. Here income mobility always means intergenerational income mobility and thus describes changes in the income level across generations. Considering two different income levels, there are four different experience groups: agents who were born into low-income families could experience either upward mobility or stay poor, and agents who were born into high-income families could experience either downward mobility or stay rich. ρ_L indicates the probability of upward mobility and $1 - \rho_H$ the probability of downward mobility.

Regarding the dynastic learning process concerning θ, π_L, and $\Delta\pi$, in line with Piketty (1995), I assume Bayesian rationality without common knowledge of Bayesian rationality. That is, dynasty i observes the behavior and experiences of other dynasties j (with $j \neq i$) in society, but takes the beliefs and experiences of j as completely exogenous and uninformative. Thus, in the updating and learning process, dynasty i does not take into account the beliefs of other agents j.[10]

[9] Note that initial beliefs may vary across families.

[10] According to Piketty (1995), including the possibility of learning from others only results in a reduction of the long-run heterogeneity of beliefs without eradicating it completely.

Initial beliefs, which are indicated by $(\mu_{i0}(\pi_L, \Delta\pi, \theta))_{i\in I}$, represent probability measures which are defined over the set of all logically possible values of π_L, $\Delta\pi$, and θ.[11] Starting in generation $t = 0$, L_0 and H_0 describe the initial income distribution in society. As before, in $t = 0$ first the effort decision is made based on initial beliefs μ_{i0} and given the tax rate τ_0. Then income y_{i0} is realized. When assuming uncertainty with regard to the main determinants of personal economic success, agents of generation $t = 0$ rationally update their beliefs based on their own experiences of income mobility. Afterwards, they transmit these updated beliefs to the next generation $t = 1$. Thus, as parents' transmitted beliefs display the child's initial beliefs, these beliefs are denoted by μ_{i1}. Last, generation $t = 0$ votes on the tax rate of generation $t = 1$, where $\tau_{i1}(\mu_{i1}(\pi_L, \Delta\pi, \theta))$ marks the individually preferred—and assumed to be socially optimal—tax rate of dynasty i.

In general, $\mu_{it}(\pi_L, \Delta\pi, \theta)$ indicates the initial beliefs of dynasty i in generation t and $\mu_{it+1}(\cdot)$ the subsequently updated beliefs. These updated beliefs are passed on to the next generation—that is, the child of dynasty i living in $t+1$—and so on for the next generations. As a result of dynastic Bayesian updating, in generation t the learning effect of dynasty i which, for example, stays in the high-income class (from $t-1$ to t) is for all $(\pi_L, \Delta\pi, \theta)$ described by:

$$\mu_{it+1}(\pi_L, \Delta\pi, \theta)$$
$$= \mu_{it}(\pi_L, \Delta\pi, \theta) \cdot \frac{\pi_L + \Delta\pi + \theta e(\theta(\mu_{it}), \tau_t)}{\sum_{\mathsf{supp}(\mu_{it})}(\pi_L' + \Delta\pi' + \theta' e(\theta(\mu_{it}), \tau_t))\mu_{it}(\pi_L', \Delta\pi', \theta')}.$$

Since Bayes' rule only puts few restrictions on short-run learning from one's own experiences, little can be said about the direction of adaption of beliefs and thus the relative weighting of individual effort and predetermined factors as crucial for economic success. Whether, for example, dynasty i ascribes more importance to effort as main factor of economic success depends on how initial beliefs interpret the event.

[11] All of these parameters are assumed to be between zero and one.

Level of Individual Effort

Individual beliefs about the role of effort and predetermined factors as crucial for personal economic success decisively influence the effort an agent is willing to invest, and the tax rate he or she prefers. When deciding as to how much effort to invest, an agent's average believed role of effort is crucial with:

$$\theta(\mu_{it}) = \sum_{\text{supp}(\mu_{it})} \theta\mu_{it}(\pi_L, \Delta\pi, \theta).$$

Thus, the agent chooses the optimal effort level:[12]

$$e_{it}(\tau_t, \theta(\mu_{it})) = \theta(\mu_{it})a\Delta y(1 - \tau_t + \gamma\Delta\pi). \tag{8.12}$$

Under uncertainty, personal effort is still independent of social origins but varies with individual beliefs about θ. Thus, the individually expected role of effort significantly influences the effort level: the more weight one puts on the role of effort as the crucial factor, the more effort one is willing to invest. Note that only if individual beliefs about θ are such that $\theta(\mu_{it}) = \theta^*$, dynasty i will choose the socially optimal effort level equivalent to the chosen effort level under certainty, as highlighted in Equation (8.8).

Individually Preferred Tax Rate

Reiterating, in the Bayesian learning process, when learning from income mobility experiences, dynasty i considers beliefs of the rest of the society to be completely uninformative. Thus, each dynasty only considers its own beliefs. However, regarding the choice of the tax rate, it is assumed that dynasty i takes into account the beliefs of the other members of society, as social beliefs display the way society responds to taxes.[13] The more society on average believes in the role of effort as crucial for economic success, the greater is the tax incentive problem. A dynasty is aware of average social beliefs which are denoted by $\overline{\theta}_t$

[12] Implicitly assuming the average believed role of effort to be equivalent to the role of effort when considering the agent's average beliefs, that is $e_{it}(\tau_t, \mu_{it}) = e_{it}(\tau_t, \theta(\mu_{it}))$.

[13] For a detailed discussion about this assumption see Piketty (1995).

and described by:

$$\overline{\theta}_t = \int_{i \in I} \theta(\mu_{it}) \, di.$$

When voting on the tax rate τ_t, the agent's choice is based on the dynasty's beliefs about the set of parameters $(\pi_L, \Delta\pi, \theta)$ as well as on the society's response to taxes. Thus, considering the average level of effort in society:

$$\overline{e}_t = (1 - \tau_t)\overline{\theta} a \Delta y + \gamma \Delta\pi \overline{\theta} a \Delta y,$$

the maximization problem of dynasty i with regard to the choice of the tax rate is as follows:

$$\tau_{it}(\mu_{it}) \in \text{argmax}_{\tau_{it} \geq 0} \sum_{\text{supp}(\mu_{it})} V_t \cdot \mu_{it}(\pi_L, \Delta\pi, \theta) \tag{8.13}$$

with

$$\begin{aligned} V_t = {} & y_L(1+\gamma) + \pi_L \Delta y (1 + \gamma(1 + \Delta\pi(\mu_{it}))) + \tau H_t \Delta\pi(\mu_{it}) \Delta y \\ & + \gamma\theta(\mu_{it}) e_{t+1} \Delta y + (1 - \tau_t + \gamma\Delta\pi(\mu_{it})) \cdot [\delta \Delta y \Delta\pi(\mu_{it}) \\ & + \overline{\theta} a \Delta y^2 (\theta(\mu_{it})(1 + \gamma\Delta\pi(\mu_{it})) - 2\overline{\theta}(1 - \tau_t + \gamma\Delta\pi(\mu_{it})))]. \end{aligned}$$

Hence, dynasty i with beliefs μ_{it} chooses the tax rate:

$$\tau_{it} = \frac{(H_t - \delta)\Delta\pi(\mu_{it})}{a \Delta y \overline{\theta}_t^2} + (1 + \gamma\Delta\pi(\mu_{it}))(1 - \frac{\theta(\mu_{it})}{\overline{\theta}_t}). \tag{8.14}$$

The individually preferred tax rate depends on the dynasty's beliefs about the extent of inequality of opportunity and the effect of effort on personal economic success. If $\theta(\mu_{it})$ *ceteris paribus* increases, the preferred tax rate of dynasty i will decrease. The more weight an agent puts on the role of effort as crucial factor, the more effort he or she is willing to invest. Thus, the agent is more averse to redistribution, as from individual perspective everyone almost gets what he/she deserves and deserves what he/she gets.

According to the first term of Equation (8.14), the demand for redistribution increases with $\Delta\pi$, as a pronounced inequality of opportunity implies high risk of failure and staying poor for children born into low-income families. The impact of inequality of opportunity on the preferences for redistribution may strengthen with dynastic altruism. Those agents who put more weight on the role of effort than average are less likely to support high levels of redistribution (and vice versa). Consequently, if individual beliefs are such that $\theta(\mu_{it}) < \overline{\theta}_t$, the two effects will run in the same direction and lower inequality of opportunity will unambiguously decrease the individually preferred tax rate. However, if individual beliefs are such that $\theta(\mu_{it}) > \overline{\theta}_t$, the two effects will be counteracting. Thus, the effect on the individually preferred tax rate is ambiguous rather than straightforward. Note that if individual beliefs regarding θ are consistent with the real marginal rate of return on effort (that is, $\theta(\mu_{it}) = \theta^*$), the individually preferred tax rate will be equivalent to the socially optimal tax rate defined above.

8.2 Social Beliefs, Inequality of Opportunity, and the Demand for Redistribution

Assuming uncertainty about the main determinants of personal economic success, different individual beliefs regarding the crucial factor for success may exist in the long run. The resulting varieties in social beliefs across countries may cause lasting differences in incentives to work and preferences for redistribution. Hence, countries with identical basic conditions can end up with completely different societies with regard to the level of redistribution, work effort, and income distribution in society. International differences will be more pronounced if countries in addition differ in the degree of dynastic altruism and in their social value judgments.

In this section initially the long-term equilibrium within society is determined. Then, assuming social beliefs to be normally distributed in the long run, the influence of both real and socially believed economic conditions on the long-term equilibrium is investigated. Finally, the efficacy of policy measures that reduce inequality of opportunity in additionally increasing intergenerational income mobility is examined.

8.2.1 Stable Beliefs and Long-Term Equilibrium

Reiterating, in the short run the direct learning effect from income mobility experiences about the main determinants of economic success is ambiguous; the updating process can go in every direction. However, in the long run indirect sampling effects counterbalance the direct learning effect.[14] Hence, agents who believe strongly in the role of effort are more represented in the high-income class than in the low-income class and vice versa. In addition, as Piketty (1995) shows, beliefs regarding the crucial factor for economic success are stable in the long run. This results from the martingale convergence theorem. In stochastic analysis, convergence can be assumed when a martingale exists. Because of the rational process of Bayesian updating, the stochastic process fulfills the martingale properties: updated beliefs of the present generation correspond to initial beliefs of the next generation. Hence, as Piketty (1995, p. 565) states, independent of initial conditions within society—L_0, H_0, τ_0 and $(\mu_{i0})_{i \in I}$—dynasty i's beliefs ($\forall i \in I$) converge toward some stationary belief $\mu_{i\infty}$ as time approaches infinity.

Assuming that dynasty i ($\forall i \in I$) puts some positive probability on the set of true parameters, that is:

$$\mu_{i0}(\pi_L^*, \Delta\pi^*, \theta^*) > 0 \quad \forall i \in I,$$

the dynasty has at least the chance to learn the truth. Otherwise, if initial beliefs should, for example, be concentrated on a single point with $\mu_{i0}(\cdot) = 1$ ($\forall i \in I$), these beliefs would be constant in the long run and any voting pattern would be steady state.

Individual beliefs regarding the determinants of personal success may change across time, depending on intergenerational income mobility experiences. However, beliefs only change as long as, given the dynasty's chosen effort, the probability of success associated with its beliefs differs from the probability regarding the true set of parameters. Put differently, for any tax rate $\tau \in [0; 1]$ as well as

[14]For more information see Piketty (1995).

for all $(\pi_L, \Delta\pi, \theta) \in \text{supp}(\mu)$ and $(\pi_L^*, \Delta\pi^*, \theta^*) \in \text{supp}(\mu)$ if:

$$\pi_L^* + \theta^* e(\theta(\mu_{it}), \tau) = \pi_L(\mu_{it}) + \theta(\mu_{it}) e(\theta(\mu_{it}), \tau), \quad \text{and} \tag{8.15}$$

$$\pi_L^* + \Delta\pi^* + \theta^* e(\theta(\mu_{it}), \tau) = \pi_L(\mu_{it}) + \Delta\pi(\mu_{it}) + \theta(\mu_{it}) e(\theta(\mu_{it}), \tau), \tag{8.16}$$

the set of beliefs $\mu(\cdot)$ will be stable in the long run.[15] There are a large number of beliefs regarding $(\pi_L, \Delta\pi, \theta)$ that fulfill the conditions (8.15) and (8.16). Hence, individual beliefs do not necessarily agree with reality to resolve the contradiction between expectation and experiences and thus to be stable in the long run. Whether a dynasty's beliefs converge to π_L^*, π_H^*, and θ^* depends on both initial beliefs and income mobility experiences. However, dynasties never gain knowledge of whether their long-term stable beliefs regarding the role of effort and predetermined factor agree with reality. Learning the truth by active experimentation is possible, but not conceivable, as this implies that a generation has to sacrifice their life supplying no effort or maximum effort. Hence, excluding the possibility of actively learning the truth, in each generation each dynasty chooses the effort level by maximizing its own private utility U_{it}.

With regard to inequality of opportunity, the conditions (8.15) and (8.16) imply:

$$\Delta\pi^* = \Delta\pi(\mu_{it}) \quad (\forall i \in I).$$

Thus, the success of society in offering equal opportunities is revealed in the long run. Hence, agents know the extent of inequality of opportunity in society and their probability of being economically successful. However, although they know that both effort and predetermined factors matter for personal success, the relative weighting of these factors is unknown.

Long-Term Tax Rate

From conditions (8.15) and (8.16) follows:

$$\pi_L^* - \pi_L(\mu_{it}) = (\theta(\mu_{it}) - \theta^*) \cdot e(\theta(\mu_{it}), \tau). \tag{8.17}$$

[15] For additional information, see Piketty (1995, p. 566).

Thus, agents who put relatively much weight on individual effort as crucial for economic success (high θ) simultaneously put relatively little weight on predetermined factors (low π). As (8.17) turns into:

$$\pi_L(\mu_{it}) = \pi_L^* + (\theta^* - \theta(\mu_{it})) \cdot e(\theta(\mu_{it}), \tau), \tag{8.18}$$

for any stable steady state, all dynasties can be ranked along a one-dimensional scale, namely their beliefs regarding the importance of predetermined factors. Thus, the politico-economic model of the median voter, as stated by Meltzer and Richard (1981), is applied. When ordering dynasties by their beliefs according to (8.18), the decisive voter is the voter with median beliefs. In addition, preferences for redistribution are single-peaked. Therefore, assuming majority rule, the elected tax rate is the median's most-preferred tax rate:

$$\tau_t = \tau_{med,t}(\mu_{med,t}).$$

Index *med* indicates the voter with median beliefs. Reiterating, beliefs converge towards some stationary beliefs $\mu_{i\infty}$ when time approaches infinity. Consequently, the equilibrium tax rate τ_t also converges towards some tax rate τ_∞ with:

$$\tau_\infty = \frac{(H_\infty - \delta)\Delta\pi^*}{a\Delta y \overline{\theta}_\infty^2} + (1 + \gamma\Delta\pi^*)(1 - \frac{\theta_{med,\infty}}{\overline{\theta}_\infty}), \tag{8.19}$$

when time approaches infinity. Here ∞ indicates long-term considerations and $\theta_{med,\infty} = \theta(\mu_{med,\infty})$. The long-term tax rate is a function increasing in H_∞ and decreasing in $\theta_{med,\infty}$. First, as an increasing share of high-income class members in society makes redistribution more effective, the tax rate increases with it. Second, if median beliefs about θ are relatively high, the support for redistributive politics and the elected tax rate will be relatively low.

When social beliefs regarding effort agree with reality (that is, $\overline{\theta}_\infty = \theta^*$), the first term of (8.19) corresponds to the socially optimal tax rate τ_∞^{opt}. This first term is independent of individual beliefs and thus is equal across all members of society. However, preferences for redistribution differ arising from varying individual beliefs regarding the determinants of success. The second term of (8.19) indicates the influence of median beliefs on its preferences of redistribution. If the median dynasty believes less strongly than average in the role of effort, it will prefer more redistribution than the dynasty with average social beliefs. In addition, all dynasties that believe more strongly in effort than the median dynasty prefer lower levels of redistribution than elected.

Long-Term Distribution of Income

In the long run, the quantity of agents belonging to the high-income class (low-income class) is stable given by H_∞ (L_∞). Consequently, the mass going out of the high-income class (low-income class) is the same as the mass coming in this class:

$$\rho_L^* L_\infty = (1 - \rho_H^*) H_\infty .$$

As $L_\infty = 1 - H_\infty$, the share of members in society receiving high income is:

$$H_\infty = \frac{\rho_L^*}{1 - \Delta\pi^*} \tag{8.20}$$

$$\text{with} \quad \rho_L^* = \pi_L^* + \theta^* \cdot \int_{i \in I} e(\tau_\infty, \theta(\mu_{it}))\, di.$$

π_L^* can be interpreted as basic probability of success. Thus, $\pi_L^* > 0$ ensures each agent some chance of economic success, independent of social origins and individual effort. The long-term share of high-income class members in society thus increases with π_L^*. The same holds true for changes in inequality of opportunity: H_∞ increases with $\Delta\pi^*$. However, favoring only children born into high-income families, social origins become more important for economic success.

The real marginal rate of return on effort, θ^*, describes the magnitude to which individual effort actually pays off. It positively affects the share of high-income class members in society. Dynasties who believe that effort plays the crucial role for economic success highly invest in effort and thus are especially in favor of a high θ^*.

Individual beliefs regarding the main determinants of economic success decisively influence their willingness to invest in effort and thus their prospects of success. Hence, social beliefs regarding the role of effort affect the income distribution in society. The more a society believes in hard work as the key factor, the more society on average invests in effort and thus the higher the share of high-income class members in society.

Level of Individual Effort

Given the long-term tax rate τ_∞, dynasty i chooses the effort level

$$e_{i\infty} = \frac{\theta(\mu_{i\infty})}{\overline{\theta}_\infty}[a\Delta y \theta_{\mathrm{med},\infty}(1+\gamma\Delta\pi^*) - \frac{(H_\infty - \delta)\Delta\pi^*}{\overline{\theta}_\infty}]. \qquad (8.21)$$

The dynasty's effort decision directly affects its probability of being economically successful. Actually, individual beliefs regarding the role of effort as the crucial factor decisively influences the willingness to invest in effort. The more strongly a dynasty believes in hard work as the crucial factor (the higher $\theta(\mu_{i\infty})$), the more effort it is willing to invest. Hence, dynasties that believe strongly in hard work as important for success display high levels of effort and are relatively averse to redistribution (and vice versa). In addition, they are more likely to succeed than dynasties that believe less strongly in hard work as the crucial factor. Consequently, as Piketty (1995) stated, dynasties that are more averse to redistribution are in steady state more represented in the high-income class than those dynasties that favor redistribution on a large scale.[16] Note that if dynasties put more weight on the role of effort than average, they will invest in effort above-average, but prefer less redistribution than socially desired.

Changes in both median beliefs and the share of high-income class members in society indirectly influence individual effort via the tax rate. A rise in the tax rate resulting from either an increase in H_∞ or a decrease in $\theta_{med,\infty}$ lowers the incentives to work. In addition to median beliefs regarding θ, average social beliefs regarding θ also indirectly affect the effort decision via the tax rate, as average beliefs display the society's respondence to taxes. However, the impact of social beliefs regarding θ on the demand for redistribution and thus incentives to work are ambiguous rather than straightforward. In addition to the other factors influencing society, below I analyze in-depth how social beliefs affect society in the long run. Moreover, whether these effects depend on the degree of dynastic altruism and social value judgment is examined.

[16] This voting pattern is the central result in Piketty (1995).

8.2.2 Influencing Factors of Long-Term Equilibrium

In the long run, agents learn the truth about their chance of experiencing income mobility and the extent of inequality of opportunity. However, the relative weighting of the determinants of personal economic success remain unknown. Thus, both the real and the socially believed role of effort decisively influence the long-term stable equilibrium in society.

Actually little is known about the distribution of individual beliefs within society. However, when investigating how society depends on real and believed social conditions, some restrictions are made about the distribution of social beliefs. In the following, individual beliefs are assumed to be normally distributed within a society in the long run. Regarding the analysis, in particular the relation of median and average social beliefs about θ are important. The results gained below are robust if uniform distribution of social beliefs is assumed. In both cases, the average and the median marginal rate of return on effort are the same. Hence, the long-term tax rate derived in (8.19) turns into:

$$\tau_\infty = \frac{(H_\infty - \delta)\Delta\pi^*}{\overline{\theta}^2_\infty a\Delta y}. \tag{8.22}$$

Assuming that $\theta_{med,\infty} = \overline{\theta}$, the long-term tax rate is equal to the tax rate under certainty except for the fact that this tax rate depends on social beliefs regarding the role of effort ($\overline{\theta}$) rather than θ^*. Thus, if $\overline{\theta}_\infty = \theta^*$, the resulting tax rate will be socially optimal. If $\overline{\theta}_\infty > \theta^*$ ($\overline{\theta}_\infty < \theta^*$), society will redistribute less (more) than socially optimal.

In the long run, based on (8.21) and assuming $\theta_{med,\infty} = \overline{\theta}_\infty$, the level of upward mobility in society is:

$$\begin{aligned}\rho^*_L &= \pi^*_L + \theta^* \cdot \int_{i\in I} e(\tau_\infty, \theta(\mu_{it}))\mathrm{d}i \\ &= \pi^*_L + \theta^*\overline{\theta}_\infty a\Delta y(1+\gamma\Delta\pi^*) - \frac{(H_\infty - \delta)\Delta\pi^*\theta^*}{\overline{\theta}_\infty}\end{aligned}$$

and thus, according to (8.20) the resulting share of high-income class members is given by:

$$H_\infty = \frac{\pi_L^* \overline{\theta}_\infty + \theta^* \overline{\theta}_\infty^2 a \Delta y (1 + \gamma \Delta\pi^*) + \delta\theta^* \Delta\pi^*}{\theta^* \Delta\pi^* + \overline{\theta}_\infty (1 - \Delta\pi^*)}. \tag{8.23}$$

Taken into account H_∞, the resulting tax rate is described by:

$$\tau_\infty = \frac{\theta^*(1 + \gamma\Delta\pi^*)\Delta\pi^*}{\overline{\theta}_\infty(1 - \Delta\pi^*) + \theta^*\Delta\pi^*} + \frac{(\pi_L^* - \delta(1 - \Delta\pi^*))\Delta\pi^*}{(\overline{\theta}_\infty(1 - \Delta\pi^*) + \theta^*\Delta\pi^*)a\Delta y \overline{\theta}_\infty} \tag{8.24}$$

and long-term effort $e_{i\infty}$ of dynasty i is:

$$e_{i\infty}(\tau_\infty, \theta(\mu_{i\infty})) = \theta(\mu_{i\infty}) \frac{(1 - \Delta\pi^*)[a\Delta y \overline{\theta}_\infty^2 (1 + \gamma\Delta\pi^*) + \delta\Delta\pi^*] - \pi_L^*\Delta\pi^*}{\overline{\theta}_\infty(\theta^*\Delta\pi^* + \overline{\theta}_\infty(1 - \Delta\pi^*))}. \tag{8.25}$$

The effects of changes in the cost parameter a on incentives to work ($e_{i\infty}$), the income distribution in society (revealed by H_∞), and the elected tax rate τ_∞ are as follows:[17]

$$\frac{\partial e_{i\infty}}{\partial a} > 0, \quad \frac{\partial H_\infty}{\partial a} > 0, \quad \text{and} \quad \frac{\partial \tau_\infty}{\partial a} < 0.$$

An increase in a enhances individual effort, as the accruing cost for one unit of effort declines. Higher levels of effort increase prospects of success and thus the share of high-income class members in society. The increasing share H_∞ of high-income class members in turn yields more demand for redistribution. Hence, the direct positive effect of a on the effort level involves indirect positive effects on H_∞ and thus the long-term tax rate. A rise in a in addition directly decreases the demand for redistribution, thus lowering the long-term tax rate. Reducing τ_∞, an increase in a indirectly effects individual effort: with a lower level of redistribution society is more willing to invest in effort. Thus, individual effort unambiguously increases with a, as it is positively affected both directly and indirectly by a rise in a. With regard to the tax rate, the indirect positive effect counteracts the direct negative effect, but the direct effect always

[17]The derivation of the effect of a on $e_{i\infty}$, H_∞ and τ_∞, as well as for all other factors considered is presented in Appendix C.4.

predominates the indirect effect. Hence, the long-term tax rate decreases with an increasing a.

The aggregate effects of changes in the income disparity between the two income levels—and thus income inequality—on $e_{i\infty}$, H_∞, and τ_∞ are the same as those effects of the cost parameter a:

$$\frac{\partial e_{i\infty}}{\partial \Delta y} > 0, \quad \frac{\partial H_\infty}{\partial \Delta y} > 0, \quad \text{and} \quad \frac{\partial \tau_\infty}{\partial \Delta y} < 0.$$

More income disparity between the two income levels incentivizes agents to invest more in effort. Higher effort levels, in turn, result in a higher share of high-income class members in society and thus more demand for redistribution. As before, the direct negative effect of Δy on τ_∞ always predominates the indirect positive effect. Hence, if income inequality increases, the long-term tax rate will decrease.

The strength of the effects that result from chances in either a or Δy depend on the underlying social value judgment and the magnitude of dynastic altruism: with regard to the level of redistribution within society, the more weight society puts on the top end of the income distribution (that is, the higher δ), the stronger is the effect of chances in a and Δy. The greater the magnitude of dynastic altruism, the stronger are the effects of a and Δy on $e_{i\infty}$ and H_∞. Consequently, the effects are smallest for a completely selfish society ($\gamma = 0$) in which a Rawlsian social welfare function ($\delta = 0$) is assumed. For simplicity, a and Δy are further normalized to one.

Dynastic Altruism

Individual effort positively affects the prospects of personal economic success and thus the expected chances of success of the next generation. Hence, incorporating the disadvantage of being born into a poor family, dynastically altruistic societies are more willing to invest in effort than completely selfish societies. By enhancing individual effort, the degree of dynastic altruism indirectly affects the income distribution and the demand for redistribution in society. Relatively high levels of individual effort in more dynastically altruistic societies yield relatively high shares of high-income class members in society and thus increases the demand for redistribution.

In addition, dynastic altruism strengthens differences in individual preferences for redistribution which result from varying beliefs regarding the crucial factor of economic success. However, as the median voter's preferences for redistribution are the same as average preferences, the elected tax rate is not directly affected by the magnitude of dynastic altruism. If the distribution of social beliefs should actually be such that $\overline{\theta}_{\infty} > \theta_{\text{med},\infty}$, the median voter would prefer more redistribution than average. In that case, the long-term tax rate would unambiguously increase with γ. Excluding this direct effect, the long-term tax rate still increases with γ because of the indirect effect via changes in individual effort. Summarizing, the effect of dynastic altruism on the resulting long-term equilibrium is as follows:[18]

$$\frac{\partial e_{i\infty}}{\partial \gamma} > 0, \quad \frac{\partial H_{\infty}}{\partial \gamma} > 0, \quad \text{and} \quad \frac{\partial \tau_{\infty}}{\partial \gamma} > 0.$$

Note that the more a dynasty incorporates the concerns of its children, the more it is willing to invest in effort and thus the higher are its prospects of success. Hence, if the degree of dynastic altruism should vary within a society, more dynastically altruistic families would be more represented in the high-income class than less altruistic families.

Varying Social Value Judgments

Social norms and values are represented in the underlying social welfare function by the value of δ. The effect of varying social norms and values on incentives to work, the income distribution, and the long-term tax rate are as follows:

$$\frac{\partial e_{i\infty}}{\partial \delta} > 0, \quad \frac{\partial H_{\infty}}{\partial \delta} > 0, \quad \text{and} \quad \frac{\partial \tau_{\infty}}{\partial \delta} < 0.$$

Social value judgment regarding the weighting of the income distribution determines the demand for redistribution. The less weight a society puts on the lower part of the income distribution (high δ), the less the desire to correct the distribution and thus the lower the tax rate. This, in turn, yields additional incentives to invest in effort. Put differently, if the concerns of the lower part

[18] The derivation of these results, as well as that of the results for the other factors considered is found in Appendix C.4.

of the income distribution are considered to be relatively important, the tax rate in society will be relatively high. In that case, individual effort is relatively low, involving a small share of the high-income class in society.

Basic Predetermined Factor

The basic predetermined factor π_L^* is independent of social origins and is identical for all members of society. Neglecting inequality of opportunity, this describes the minimum chance to become a member of the high-income class independent of the individual effort choice. Changes in the basic predetermined factor affect $e_{i\infty}$, H_∞, and τ_∞ as follows:

$$\frac{\partial e_{i\infty}}{\partial \pi_L^*} < 0, \quad \frac{\partial H_\infty}{\partial \pi_L^*} > 0, \quad \text{and} \quad \frac{\partial \tau_\infty}{\partial \pi_L^*} > 0.$$

Across society, the share of high-income class members increases with π_L^*, as for all members of society the chance of being successful increases.[19] This positive direct effect on H_∞ induces the long-term tax rate to increase and thus individual effort to decrease, as higher taxes cause rising disincentives. The indirect negative effect of a rise in π_L^* on the willingness to invest in effort reinforces its direct effect: in society, personal economic success is more based on predetermined factors and luck than self-determined.

Real Role of Effort

The real marginal rate of return on effort, which is unknown in the long run, directly affects individual prospects of success. With an increase in θ^* individual effort pays off more yielding the probability of achieving y_H to increase and thus the share of high-income class members in society. This rise in H_∞ causes the long-term tax rate to increase and thus individual effort to decrease. Consequently, with uncertainty about the precise role of effort, individual effort decreases, although one unit of effort is more valuable for personal economic success.[20] Again, the reduction in $e_{i\infty}$ brings along indirect effects on H_∞ and τ_∞. Even though a rise in θ^* indirectly decreases H_∞, the direct positive effect always predominates. Consequently, for all plausible value ranges, the

[19]Note that the members of society cannot observe this changes in π_L^*.

[20]Note that the level of individual effort is not directly affected by changes in θ^*, as such changes are not observed by the individuals within society.

influence of θ^* on $e_{i\infty}$, H_∞, and τ_∞ is as follows (for the derivation of this, see Appendix C.4):

$$\frac{\partial e}{\partial \theta^*} < 0, \quad \frac{\partial H}{\partial \theta^*} > 0, \quad \text{and} \quad \frac{\partial \tau}{\partial \theta^*} > 0.$$

Neither the size of dynastic altruism nor different social value judgments change the sign of the aggregate effect of the real marginal rate of return on effort θ^* on the resulting long-term equilibrium in society. Surprisingly, the impact of the real marginal rate of return on effort θ^* is the same as the impact of the basic predetermined factor π_L^*. The demand for redistribution enhances with both θ^* and π_L^*, simultaneously narrowing incentives to work.

Socially Believed Role of Effort

Individual beliefs regarding the role of effort as crucial for success significantly influence the individual's willingness to invest in effort and his or her preferences for redistribution. At the aggregate level, social beliefs are crucial, as decisively affecting average effort and the level of redistribution in society. Here if $\overline{\theta}_\infty = \theta^*$, the society will on average choose the optimal effort level and elect the socially optimal tax rate. However, if $\overline{\theta}_\infty > \theta^*$ ($\overline{\theta}_\infty < \theta^*$), the society will over-invest (under-invest) in effort and redistribute less (more) than is socially optimal.

The more weight society puts on effort as the main determinant of economic success, the more its members are willing to invest. Simultaneously, as the income distribution is noticed to be quite just, the demand for redistribution is relatively low. Rising $\overline{\theta}_\infty$, both direct effects, the positive effect on $e_{i\infty}$ and the negative effect on τ_∞, bring along several indirect—partially counteracting—effects which were described in detail earlier. Hence, the aggregate effect of $\overline{\theta}_\infty$ on incentives to work, the demand for redistribution, and income distribution in society is ambiguous, significantly depending on social objectives. If the share to which the needs of children born into high-income class members are considered in the social welfare function does not exceed the threshold value

δ^* with:[21]

$$\delta^* = \frac{\pi_L^*}{1-\Delta\pi^*} + \frac{\theta^*\overline{\theta}_\infty^2(1+\gamma\Delta\pi^*)}{2\overline{\theta}_\infty(1-\Delta\pi^*)+\theta^*\Delta\pi^*},$$

both direct effects will outweigh the possibly counteracting indirect effects. Hence, for $\delta < \delta^*$ with a rising $\overline{\theta}_\infty$ individual and average effort in society increases, while the chosen tax rate decreases. Thus, the share of high-income class members in society additionally increases. Summed up, if $\delta < \delta^*$, the aggregate effects will be such that:

$$\frac{\partial e_{i\infty}}{\partial\overline{\theta}_\infty} > 0, \quad \frac{\partial H_\infty}{\partial\overline{\theta}_\infty} > 0, \quad \text{and} \quad \frac{\partial\tau_\infty}{\partial\overline{\theta}_\infty} < 0.$$

Otherwise, for a sufficiently high δ (with $\delta > \delta^*$) the tax rate increases with $\overline{\theta}_\infty$ causing individual and average effort to decrease. For all plausible value ranges, the aggregate effect on H_∞ is left unchanged, still increasing with $\overline{\theta}$ (as shown in Appendix C.4).

The threshold value δ^* depends on real and socially believed economic conditions. In addition, this threshold value increases with the size of dynastic altruism. Consequently, given social value judgments, in more dynastically altruistic societies it is more likely that with an increasing $\overline{\theta}_\infty$ individual willingness to invest in effort increases and simultaneously the demand for redistribution decreases.

Contrary to the real role of effort, social beliefs putting relatively much weight on effort as the crucial factor for economic success likely provide large incentives to work and less support for redistribution. Therefore, except for a sufficiently high δ, the impact of the real role and the socially believed role of effort on incentives to work and the demand of redistribution in society are opposing. However, if society puts relatively much weight on the concerns of the top end of society ($\delta > \delta^*$), even an increase in $\overline{\theta}_\infty$ will lead to disincentives to work and demand for redistribution on a large scale.

[21]The derivation of the threshold value δ^* is shown in Appendix C.4.

Inequality of Opportunity

Indicating social origins, parental income influences a child's opportunities and thus his or her prospects of success. If there is great inequality of opportunity, children born into low-income families will be strongly disadvantaged compared to children born into high-income families. In that case, society favors an extensive welfare state, as the income distribution in society is regarded to be quite unfair. In favor of children born into high-income families, greater inequality of opportunity increases their relative chance of achieving the high-income level. The share of high-income class members in society increases. In addition, in dynastic altruistic societies parent's willingness to invest in effort rises with greater inequality of opportunity, as they consider that in this case the child suffers more strongly from a poor family background. Hence, the extent of inequality of opportunity directly affects the equilibrium tax rate, the income distribution in society, and possibly incentives to work. These direct effects bring along several indirect effects. First, if inequality of opportunity is reduced, social origins will become less important for economic success. Thus, income is distributed more fairly across society, decreasing the demand for redistribution. In that case, as the tax incentive problem becomes less important, individual effort increases involving an increase in H_{∞}. Second, greater equality of opportunity decreases the relatively higher chance of being successful for children born into high-income families. This reduces the share of high-income class members in society. As a result, the tax rate decreases and thus incentives to work increase. Third, in dynastically altruistic societies, reducing inequality of opportunity additionally lowers individual effort, as the potential disadvantage of the next generation due to unequal opportunity is less serious. Lower levels of individual and average effort decrease the share of high-income class members in society. Consequently, this reduces the equilibrium tax rate.

With regard to the long-term tax rate, both direct and indirect effects of greater equality of opportunity go in the same direction. Thus, diminishing inequality of opportunity unambiguously decreases the elected tax rate, as:

$$\frac{\partial \tau_{\infty}}{\partial \Delta \pi^*} > 0.$$

However, the aggregate effect of changes in inequality of opportunity on incentives to work is ambiguous. In first place, it depends on the relation of the real and the socially believed marginal rate of return on effort weighted by $\Delta\pi^{*2}$ and $(1-\Delta\pi^*)^2$, respectively. If social beliefs about θ are sufficiently low compared to the real role of effort—that is, for $\overline{\theta}_\infty < \theta^*(\frac{\Delta\pi^*}{1-\Delta\pi^*})^2$—the indirect negative effects predominate the direct positive effect. In this case, reducing inequality of opportunity always increases individual effort, as:

$$\frac{\partial e_{i\infty}}{\partial \Delta\pi^*} < 0.$$

Whether this holds for $\overline{\theta}_\infty > \theta^*(\frac{\Delta\pi^*}{1-\Delta\pi^*})^2$, depends on both the size of dynastic altruism and social value judgments in society. Only if:[22]

$$\delta\frac{1}{\overline{\theta}_\infty} + \gamma\overline{\theta}_\infty < \frac{\pi_L^* + \theta^*\overline{\theta}_\infty}{\overline{\theta}_\infty(1-\Delta\pi^*)^2 - \theta^*\Delta\pi^{*2}},$$

will effort still increase with $\Delta\pi^*$. Put differently, if dynastic altruism is pronounced and/or society is highly concerned about the top end of the income distribution, greater equality of opportunity will set disincentives to work.

The aggregate effect of inequality of opportunity on the income distribution in society is also ambiguous. Here whether H_∞ rises with $\Delta\pi^*$ crucially depends on the relation between $\overline{\theta}_\infty$ and θ^*. Primarily, the positive effects (consisting of the direct effect and the indirect effect via effort) outweigh the negative indirect tax-induced effect. For example, if society puts on average equal or more weight on the role of effort than is actually the case, greater equality of opportunity will always decrease the share of high-income class members in society, as

$$\frac{\partial H_\infty}{\partial \Delta\pi^*} > 0.$$

[22] The derivation of the aggregate effect and the threshold of δ and γ are shown in Appendix C.4.

Table 8.1: Effect on Long-Term Equilibrium

	Demand for Redistribution	Incentives to Work	Share of High-Income Class Members
Dynastic Altruism	+	+	+
Social Objectives	−	+	−
Basic Predetermined Factor	+	−	+
Real Role of Effort	+	−	+
Socially Believed Role of Effort	−[a]	+[a]	−
Inequality of Opportunity	+	−[b]	+[c]

[a] This is fulfilled only if $\delta < \delta^*$. Otherwise, the effects are opposing.
[b] This is fulfilled expect if for $\overline{\theta}_\infty > \theta^*(\frac{\Delta\pi^*}{1\ \ \Delta\pi^*})^2$ it holds that $\delta\frac{1}{\overline{\theta}_\infty} + \gamma\overline{\theta}_\infty < \frac{\pi_L^* + \theta^*\overline{\theta}_\infty}{\overline{\theta}_\infty(1\ \ \Delta\pi^*)^2\ \ \theta^*\Delta\pi^{*2}}$. Then, the effect is opposing.
[c] This is fulfilled expect if for $\overline{\theta}_\infty < \theta^*$ it holds that $\delta + \gamma\overline{\theta}_\infty^2 < \frac{\pi_L^* + \theta^*\overline{\theta}_\infty}{\theta^*\overline{\theta}_\infty} \cdot (\theta^* - \overline{\theta}_\infty)$. Then, the effect is opposing.

This will hold true for $\overline{\theta}_\infty < \theta^*$ if γ and/or δ are sufficiently high—that is, if:[23]

$$\gamma\overline{\theta}_\infty^2 + \delta > (1 + \frac{\pi_L^*}{\theta^*\overline{\theta}_\infty})(\theta^* - \overline{\theta}_\infty).$$

In sum, if the average believed role of effort is higher than is actually the case, society on average over-invests in effort. In that case, reducing inequality of opportunity unambiguously decreases the share of high-income class members in society. Whether for $\overline{\theta} < \theta^*$ greater equality of opportunity increases or decreases the share of high-income class members in society depends on the magnitude of dynastic altruism and the social objective. Here only if dynastic altruism is less pronounced and the underlying social welfare function is prone to a Rawlsian social welfare function, will greater equality of opportunity increase the share of high-income class members in society. Summarizing, Table 8.1 shows an overview of the results gained.

8.2.3 Equality of Opportunity and Income Mobility

Although greater equality of opportunity unambiguously reduces the support for redistribution, its effect on incentives to work and the income distribution

[23]For the derivation of this see Appendix C.4.

in society is ambiguous. For example, if society puts relatively much weight on effort as the crucial factor and dynastic altruism is well pronounced, reducing inequality of opportunity will set disincentives to work and the share of high-income class members will decrease. In addition to predetermined factors such as inequality of opportunity, the willingness to invest in effort significantly influences prospects of success and thus the chance of respective upward and downward mobility. In the following, whether policy measures that promote greater equality of opportunity also increases intergenerational income mobility is investigated.

Prospects of Social Advancement

In the long run, the average probability of upward mobility within a society is defined by:

$$\overline{\rho}_L^* = \pi_L^* + \theta^* \cdot \overline{e}(\overline{\theta}) = \pi_L^* + \theta^* \frac{(1-\Delta\pi^*)[\overline{\theta}_\infty^2(1+\gamma\Delta\pi^*) + \delta\Delta\pi^*] - \pi_L^*\Delta\pi^*}{\overline{\theta}_\infty(1-\Delta\pi^*) + \theta^*\Delta\pi^*}.$$

Analogously, the average probability of downward mobility is:

$$1 - \overline{\rho}_H^* = 1 - \Delta\pi^* - \overline{\rho}_L^*.$$

Except for the prevalent inequality of opportunity, the other factors influencing society—γ, δ, π_L^*, θ^*, and $\overline{\theta}_\infty$—positively affect the probability of upward mobility and negatively influences the risk of downward mobility in society. Although the aggregate effect is the same, the causality is rather different. As incentives to work increases with the size of dynastic altruism, the chance of upward mobility increases. Regarding social value judgments, the more weight society puts on the top end of the income distribution, the lower its support for redistributive policies. Thus, as individual effort increases with a decreasing tax rate, probability of upward mobility increases and probability of downward mobility decreases. For all children of a society, prospects of success increase with the basic predetermined factor π_L^* thus increasing $\overline{\rho}_L^*$ and decreasing $1 - \overline{\rho}_H^*$. Here the increase in π_L^* and the accompanying decrease in effort yield a steady state that is more based on predetermined factors and luck than self-determined. The aggregate effect of both the real role and the socially believed role of effort on the probability of mobility in society is not straightforward. A multitude of direct and indirect effects exist, often counteracting each other. However, as shown in Appendix C.4, an increase in both θ^* and $\overline{\theta}_\infty$ unambiguously increases prospects of social advancement and decreases the risk of downward social movement.

Whether policy measures that promote greater equality of opportunity also enhance prospects of social advancement critically depends on their effects on incentives to work. Thus, it is dependent on social beliefs regarding the role of effort, as well as on the magnitude of dynastic altruism and the social objective. If the socially believed role of effort is sufficiently small related to θ^* and weighted by $\Delta\pi^*$ (precisely, for $\overline{\theta} \leq \theta^*(\frac{\Delta\pi^*}{1-\Delta\pi^*})^2$), more equality of opportunity will always increase the prospects of social advancement, as:

$$\frac{\partial \overline{\rho}_L^*}{\partial \Delta\pi^*} < 0.$$

However, if average social beliefs are such that $\overline{\theta} > \theta^*(\frac{\Delta\pi^*}{1-\Delta\pi^*})^2$, it will depend on the magnitude of dynastic altruism and social value judgments whether greater equality of opportunity increase the chance of upward mobility. In that case, only if:[24]

$$\gamma\overline{\theta}_\infty + \delta < \frac{\pi_L^* + \theta^*\overline{\theta}_\infty}{\overline{\theta}_\infty(1-\Delta\pi^*)^2 - \theta^*\Delta\pi^{*2}}$$

policy measure that reduce inequality of opportunity will additionally increase the probability of upward mobility. Put another way, if dynastic altruism is pronounced and/or society has a relatively large concern about children born into high-income families, will greater equality of opportunity decrease the chance of social advancement.

Intergenerational Income Mobility

In the long run, the part of society that experiences upward mobility is equal to the part that experiences downward mobility. The mobile part of society is described by M and is given by:

$$M \equiv 2 \cdot \overline{\rho}_L^* \cdot L_\infty = 2 \cdot \overline{\rho}_L^* \cdot (1 - H_\infty)$$

[24]The derivation for this is shown in Appendix C.4.

Assuming $\gamma = \delta = 0$, if:[25]

$$\overline{\theta}_{\infty} < \overline{\theta}_M = \theta^*(1 + \frac{1}{1 - \Delta\pi^*}),$$

income mobility will increase with greater equality of opportunity (that is, $\frac{\partial M}{\partial \Delta\pi^*} < 0$). Hence, even in this simple case greater equality of opportunity does not unambiguously increase intergenerational income mobility. In addition to economic conditions, it crucially depends on social beliefs regarding the role of effort as crucial for success. If society puts relatively much weight on effort as the main determinant of economic success compared to the real marginal rate of return on effort, a reduction in inequality of opportunity will yield less mobility within society. As a consequence, if social beliefs regarding the role of effort do not exceed the upper bound denoted by $\overline{\theta}_M$, intergenerational income mobility increases with greater equality of opportunity. As can be formally seen in Appendix C.4, dynastic altruism unambiguously enhances intergenerational income mobility, as does a rise in δ. However, the magnitude of dynastic altruism lowers the upper bound and thus, the critical value of $\overline{\theta}_M$. Consequently, in more dynastically altruistic societies, it is less likely that intergenerational income mobility increases with greater equality of opportunity. The same holds when δ increases.

8.3 Implications

With uncertainty about the main determinants of personal economic success, individual beliefs regarding the respective role of self-determined and exogenously determined factors crucially influence incentives to work and the demand for redistribution. These individual beliefs emerge—and change across time—due to personal income mobility experiences. In this context the present chapter examines how both real and socially believed economic conditions affect society in the long run.[26] Crucially, social beliefs regarding self-determination and exogenous determination may be accountable for international differences in incentives to work, the support for redistribution, and thus income inequality. In addition, these social beliefs affect intergenerational income mobility.

[25] For the derivation of this see Appendix C.4.

[26] Table 8.1 presents the majority of the results gained.

Actually, the real marginal rate of return on effort defines how valuable effort is for being economically successful. However, as this real role of effort is unknown in society, beliefs regarding the role of effort decisively determine the amount of effort invested. If society puts significantly much weight on effort as the crucial factor, most likely its members will be more willing to invest in effort and will oppose redistribution on a large scale. Necessary to that end is that the social objective cover the need of the least well-off in society sufficiently strongly.

On the contrary, the long-term tax rate increases with the real marginal rate of return on effort. Thus, this lowers incentives to work, although one unit of effort is more valuable.[27] Changes in the basic predetermined factor yield the same effects as the real role of effort. Hence, with uncertainty regarding the main determinants of economic success, whether indeed self-determined or exogenously determined factors increase does not change the result. In both cases, members of society notice enhanced prospects of success and thus an increasing share of high-income class members without knowing by what this is caused. As a consequence, raising the real chance of success increases redistribution and thus lowers income inequality. However, as an increasing tax rate decreases individual effort, exogenously determined factors become relatively more important. Therefore, income distribution is seen to be quite unfair.

Consequently, a rise in the real marginal rate of return on effort is not as advantageous as is affecting social beliefs in favor of effort as the crucial factor. In both cases, social economic prosperity increases. However, contrary to the socially believed role of effort, a rise in the real role of effort lowers incentives to work, yielding an income distribution that is highly unfair. Summing up, optimism regarding the importance of hard work for being economically successful is beneficial in enhancing incentives to work and thus the prospects of economic success. Simultaneously, this lowers support for redistributive policies.

Regarding dynastic altruism, the willingness to invest in effort increases with its magnitude. Therefore, if the magnitude of dynastic altruism varies within a society, more dynastically altruistic families will be more represented in high-

[27]Note that with uncertainty about the real role of effort, changes in this real marginal rate of return on effort only indirectly affect incentives to work.

income classes than dynasties with less marked dynastic altruism. The demand for redistribution additionally increases with dynastic altruism. Consequently, the degree of dynastic altruism in society positively affects incentives to work and the level of redistribution, thus lowering income inequality. In addition, in these societies income distribution tends to be more fairly distributed.

How society succeeds in offering equal opportunities is crucial for prospects of success, incentives to work, and the demand for redistribution. The more society promotes greater equality of opportunity, the more just is the income distribution in society and thus the lower the demand for redistribution. However, the effect of greater equality of opportunity on incentives to work and the income distribution in society is ambiguous. Whether effort, for example, increases with greater equality of opportunity critically depends on social beliefs regarding the role of effort, as well as on the magnitude of dynastic altruism and the value judgment in society. If society does not believe sufficiently in the role of effort, policy measures that reduce inequality of opportunity will increase the willingness to invest in effort and thus will enhance the prospects of social advancement in society. However, if society believes sufficiently strongly in effort, in societies with pronounced dynastic altruism for example, greater equality of opportunity will yield low incentives to work. Thus, decreasing effort reduces the chance of upward mobility.

In addition to the prevalent inequality of opportunity, the willingness to invest in effort significantly influences an individual's prospects of success and thus the degree of intergenerational income mobility. Whether policy measures that reduce inequality of opportunity also increase intergenerational income mobility decisively depends on social beliefs regarding the role of effort. Policy measures promoting greater equality of opportunity will simultaneously increase intergenerational income mobility only if society puts relatively little weight on effort. In societies with pronounced dynastic altruism, it is less likely that such measures additionally increase intergenerational income mobility.

Reiterating, optimism about the importance of hard work set incentives to work. However, aiming to reduce inequality of opportunity, too much optimism lowers the likelihood of success in society and sets disincentives to work. In that case, reducing inequality of opportunity simultaneously decreases intergenerational income mobility. According to the American dream, everyone can make it from rags to riches.[28] This illustrates the widespread optimism in the United States regarding hard work as the key factor for personal economic success. Compared to countries like Germany, the United States tends to put more weight on effort as the crucial factor for economic success. Confirming the results gained in this theory-based chapter, the U.S. population is less in favor of an extensive welfare state than is Germany. Beyond the existing literature, the study in this chapter states that optimism regarding the importance of hard work reduces the probability of increasing intergenerational income mobility when greater equality of opportunity is promoted. In fact, although the U.S. population puts more weight on effort as the crucial factor, Germany tends to be more mobile.

[28] There is a large body of literature dealing with "American exceptionalism". The literature regarding the theory of U.S. exceptionalism goes back to Tocqueville.

Chapter 9

Income Mobility and Preferences for Redistribution: Empirical Observations

There is a growing body of literature questioning the proposition that solely the relative position in the income distribution determines individual preferences for redistribution as stated by Meltzer and Richard (1981). Hence, it is questionable whether individuals with relatively low pre-tax income indeed support high levels of redistribution (and vice versa). The theory-based literature demonstrates that the demand for redistribution is not necessarily outcome oriented, but may include, for example, the need for fairness and equity.[1] In addition, according to Piketty (1995) and the theory-based study in Chapter 8, past income history is important for individual preferences with respect to redistributive policies. Experiencing income mobility positively affects individual beliefs regarding hard work as crucial for personal economic success. In this case, putting more weight on self-determined than on exogenously determined factors causes the individual demand for redistribution to decrease. Consequently, individuals who have experienced upward mobility will less likely support relatively high levels of redistribution (and vice versa). The aim of this chapter is to examine whether the empirical literature finds evidence for this pattern.

When looking at income mobility as influencing factor of the demand for redistribution, both experiences and expectations of upward mobility are important and thus find consideration in the economic literature. According to theory, both prospective and retrospective, rising income increases the demand for redistribution, but the causality is rather different. Mostly related to Chapter 8, this chapter focuses on the effect of past income experiences.[2]

[1] For more information see, for example, Alesina and Giuliano (2011).

[2] Concentrating on expectations rather than experiences of income mobility, Benabou and Ok (2001), Fong (2006), and Rainer and Siedler (2008), for example, find evidence that the expectation of rising future income decreases the demand for redistribution.

The studies of Corneo (2001) and Corneo and Grüner (2002) estimate the effect of beliefs regarding the role of effort on individual preferences for redistribution. Even though *a priori* an individual's income level and his or her preferences for redistribution are not linked, such an link may emerge due to individual beliefs. This effect is called public values effect. In addition, both studies examine the Meltzer-Richard hypothesis, focusing on the effect of pecuniary advantage.[3] Using data from the *International Social Survey Programme* (ISSP), both studies find cross-national evidence for the Meltzer-Richard hypothesis. Thus, in all countries considered—including the United States and West Germany—the demand for redistribution decreases considerably with increasing income level. However, whether the public values effect significantly influences preferences for redistribution depends on the respective country. For example, Corneo (2001) demonstrates that when deciding about the level of redistribution, the West German population includes collective concerns, whereas in the United States predominantly pecuniary advantage is considered.[4]

Using U.S. data from 1998 *Gallup Poll Social Audit Survey*, Fong (2001) shows that beliefs regarding the main determinants of economic success, whether putting more weight on self- or exogenously determined factors, significantly influence the support for redistribution. However, according to her, most likely this is because of reciprocity or equity concerns rather the tax incentives. In addition, Fong (2001) examines the relevance of altruism. As she demonstrates, altruism may indeed be crucial, as perceiving more poverty increases the support for redistribution. Hence, this reinforces the assumption made in Chapter 8 that some societies are dynastically altruistic, thus caring about the well-being of their offspring.

Also focusing on the United States, Alesina and La Ferrara (2005) empirically estimate the influence of past income mobility experiences on individual attitude towards redistribution. Using data from the *General Social Survey* (GSS), they find evidence that beliefs regarding the crucial factor for personal

[3]For completeness, they investigate a third effect, namely social rivalry, stating that an individual's relative standard of living influences his or her preferences for redistribution.

[4]A review on the recent literature on this topic is provided by Corneo (2004). In addition, a further strand of literature addresses the issue of whether preferences for redistribution are affected by the political system, where West and East Germany can be seen as a natural experiment. Here see, for example, Alesina and Fuchs-Schündeln (2007) and Pfarr, Schmid, and Ulrich (2013).

economic success affect individual preferences for redistribution. Hence, individuals who strongly believe in self-determined factors as crucial for success are more averse to redistribution (and vice versa). In addition, they investigate the influence of general mobility as present in society. Here, they show that measures considering expected gains and losses from redistribution perform better than general mobility in explaining individual attitudes towards redistribution.

In a cross-national comparison over 33 countries, based on data from ISSP, Guillaud (2013) confirms the importance of experiencing upward mobility for individual preferences for redistribution. Individuals who experienced upward mobility tend to oppose redistribution, whereas those who have moved downward more likely favor it. Also basing on ISSP data, Kuhn (2013) analyzes the demand for redistribution as existing in Germany. Accordingly, individuals who experiences upward mobility regarding their social status prefer more equally distributed wages than the perceived distribution.

Recently, focusing on Germany, Pfarr (2012) empirically examined the Meltzer-Richard hypothesis and Piketty's learning model. In his study, rather than using survey data, preferences for redistribution are revealed by a discrete choice experiment.[5] Pfarr shows that while eliciting preferences contradicts the Meltzer-Richard model, data strongly support Piketty's learning model.

[5]According to Pfarr (2012), using survey data one cannot differentiate between the demand and the supply side. Thus, such survey data are not able to predict individuals' decision making under the restriction of a budget constraint.

Chapter 10

Conclusions

According to Piketty (1995), supporters of left-wing parties—characterized by favoring an extensive welfare state—are more represented in low-income classes and less represented in high-income classes. This voting pattern arises because of varying individual beliefs regarding the determinants of personal economic success. Individuals who put relatively much weight on self-determined rather than exogenously determined factors invest much in effort. In addition, they are more averse to redistributive policies than those putting more weight on exogenously determined factors.

Going one step further, Chapter 8 examined the long-term impact of both real and socially believed economic conditions on incentives to work and the demand for redistribution in society. Raising the real marginal rate of return on effort unambiguously increases the tax rate and thus incentives to work decrease.[1] As decreasing effort increases the weight of exogenously determined factors, income tends to be less fairly distributed. Contrarily, if society puts more weight on effort as the crucial factor, incentives to work will most likely increase and the demand for redistribution will decrease. Necessary to that end is that society is sufficiently concerned about its least well-off members.

As illustrated in Chapter 9, empirical studies confirm that social beliefs regarding the determinants of economic success significantly influence individual attitudes towards redistribution. However, how much preferences for redistribution actually depend on individual beliefs regarding the role of effort and how much they are influenced by pecuniary advantage varies across countries. Based on a discrete choice experiment, Pfarr (2012) highlights the importance of individual beliefs in explaining individual preferences for redistribution in Germany. However, according to his study, the individual position in the in-

[1] This results from the fact that the members of society only notice enhanced prospects of success without knowing where this comes from and thus incentives to work are not directly affected.

come distribution seems to be rather insignificant for German preferences for redistribution.

Further factors such as altruism may be important in explaining preferences for redistribution.[2] Considering dynastic altruism, it turns out that dynastically altruistic societies exhibit enhanced incentives to work as the advantage for the next generation thereby induced is taken into account. In addition, these societies are less averse to redistributive policies. Thus, if the degree of dynastic altruism varies within a society, more dynastically altruistic families will be more represented in high-income classes than dynasties with less pronounced dynastic altruism. Hence, the voting pattern stated by Piketty (1995) is mitigated by varying dynastic altruism within society.

The prevalent inequality of opportunity, displaying the disadvantage of being born into a poor family, decisively influences the society's valuation of the income distribution. Hence, the more a society succeeds in offering equal opportunities, the more averse are its members to redistribution, since income seems to be fairly distributed. However, the impact of greater equality of opportunity on incentives to work turns out to be ambiguous, critically depending on the socially believed role of effort. If society believes insufficiently less in the role of effort, greater equality of opportunity will always increase the willingness to invest in effort, enhancing individual prospects of social advancement. However, if social beliefs regarding effort surpass a threshold level and dynastic altruism is well pronounced, for example, individual effort decreases with greater equality of opportunity decreasing the chance of upward mobility.

As it results, in addition to inequality of opportunity, the prevalent intergenerational income mobility critically depends on the society's willingness to work. In fact, social beliefs regarding the role of effort decisively influence individual effort and thus intergenerational income mobility. It turns out that only if society believes insufficiently in effort as the crucial factor, policy measures that promote greater equality of opportunity will simultaneously increase income mobility. In addition, the probability of increasing intergenerational income mobility when promoting greater equality of opportunity declines with the degree of dynastic altruism.

[2]Fong (2001) illustrates that altruism generally influences individual preferences for redistribution.

Summarizing, optimism regarding the importance of hard work is favorable for setting incentives to work. However, when aiming to reduce inequality of opportunity, optimism on a large scale may reduce the probability of success and set disincentives to work. In that case, such policy measures promoting greater equality of opportunity may simultaneously decrease intergenerational income mobility. Consequently, if the members of society have experienced enhanced upward mobility in the past, prompting them to believe strongly in effort, this optimism may at present yield a lower income mobility.

As indicated by the myth of the American dream, the U.S. population believes strongly in hard work as the key factor for economic success. As shown in Chapter 8, these beliefs may explain the U.S. population's aversion to redistribution on a large scale. Hence, although income inequality is higher in the United States, its population is more averse to an extensive welfare state than in Germany. Favoring lower levels of redistribution, in the United States incomes remain less equally distributed. However, as income distribution is regarded to be quite fair, the demand for redistribution remains low. Beyond the existing literature, the theory-based study in Chapter 8 demonstrates that in societies with pronounced optimism regarding the importance of hard work, it is less likely that intergenerational income mobility will increase when promoting greater equality of opportunity. This may explain why the United States tends to be less mobile than Germany, although social beliefs prompt the U.S. population to invest highly in personal effort.

Final Remarks

Family background plays an important role for individual prospects of success. That is, income levels are to some degree persistent across generations. However, this is disadvantageous for society in many respects. The aim of this thesis was to examine when policy measures that aim to reduce economic inequality and/or promote greater equality of opportunity are successful in increasing intergenerational income mobility.

Part I of this thesis covers education policy and how it influences intergenerational income mobility within society. Public education can be understood as intergenerational transfer payment with a redistributive impact. This affects children's prospects of success and thus income mobility across generations. In addition to promoting greater equality of opportunity, state education investment tends to increase a child's human capital. However, public education also decisively influences parents' decision on how much to invest in a child's human capital. Thus, whether public education increase intergenerational income mobility critically depends on how public and private human capital investment influence each other. If these two are substitutes, education policy does increase intergenerational income mobility, which is not the case if the two forms of investments complement each other.

The importance of human capital accumulation is illustrated not only theoretically, but also empirically, demonstrating that education crucially affects the strength of the economic parent-child connection. As the key factor of the intergenerational transmission of economic advantage in Germany, education is accountable for 20 percent of the observed intergenerational income immobility, which is measured by the intergenerational income elasticity. However, parental influence operates through many rather than a single channel. In second place, about 15 percent of the intergenerational immobility is attributed to occupation. This pattern does not seem to be confined to Germany. In fact, international comparison reveals that education and occupation are the most important factors of intergenerational transmission in the United States and Great Britain, as well.[1]

As redistributive policy measures that reduce economic inequality, public education does not necessarily enhance intergenerational income mobility. Only measures that weaken the economic parent-child connection achieve this goal. This can either be effected by reducing parental influence or by decreasing earnings' return on human capital investment. Consequently, diminishing the importance of family background, education policy will increase intergenerational mobility if public education crowds out private human capital investment.

Part II, capturing the issue whether policy measures that promote greater equality of opportunity also increase income mobility, addresses their dependence on social beliefs regarding the main determinants of economic success. If the main determinants of economic success are uncertain, individual beliefs regarding these determinants will emerge due to personal intergenerational income mobility experiences. Actually international differences with regard to supporting redistributive measures can be explained by varying social beliefs across countries, which additionally significantly influence incentives to work.

Social optimism regarding the importance of hard work promotes efficiency by setting incentives to work. However, when reducing inequality of opportunity such optimism on a large scale may cause disincentives to work.[2] This decreases the probability of economic success. Both prevalent inequality of opportunity and a society's willingness to invest in effort decisively influence intergenerational income mobility within society. Thus whether measures promoting greater equality of opportunity increase or decrease intergenerational income mobility critically depends on social beliefs regarding the role of effort. It turns out that only if society's belief in the role of effort is weak policy measures that promote greater equality of opportunity will simultaneously increase income mobility. Consequently, if the members of society have experienced enhanced upward mobility in the past, their strong belief in effort may at present cause lower income mobility.

[1]The results for Great Britain and the United States are taken from Blanden et al. (2014).

[2]In dynastic altruistic societies, reducing inequality of opportunity directly lowers incentives to work, as the disadvantage of the next generation of being born into a low-income family decreases.

Summing up, generations are connected through various channels. Two of these, namely education and individual beliefs regarding self-determination rather than exogenous determination, are examined in this thesis. Both have to be considered in designing public policies. As a general result, policy measures that offer more equal opportunities in society only increase intergenerational income mobility if the strength of the economic parent-child connection is simultaneously reduced. With regard to public education, this is achieved if public education yields a decline in private human capital investment. The same holds true if beliefs regarding self-determination are less pronounced, as the individual level of effort, which critically depends on family beliefs persisting across generations, is less important.

Regarding the observed increase in income inequality in many industrialized countries, high levels of mobility across generations became considerably more important. Policy measures which redistribute income may also have an impact on equality of opportunity. In fact, intergenerational income mobility does not necessarily increase with such measures. When aiming to further increase intergenerational income mobility, this thesis gave more insight on how this could be achieved.

References

Alesina, A., & Angeletos, G.-M. (2005). Fairness and Redistribution. *American Economic Review*, *95*(4), 960-980. (Reprinted in Fairness in Law and Economics, edited by L. A. Fennell and R. H. McAdams)

Alesina, A., & Fuchs-Schündeln, N. (2007). Good-Bye Lenin (or Not?): The Effect of Communism on People's Preferences. *American Economic Review*, *97*(4), 1507-1528.

Alesina, A., & Giuliano, P. (2011). Preferences for redistribution. In A. Bisin & J. Benhabib (Eds.), *Handbook of Social Economics* (p. 93-132). North Holland.

Alesina, A., & Glaeser, E. L. (2004). *Fighting Poverty in the US and Europe.* Oxford: Oxford University Press.

Alesina, A., & La Ferrara, E. (2005). Preferences for redistribution in the land of opportunities. *Journal of Public Economics*, *89*, 897-931.

Atkinson, A. B., & Piketty, T. (2007). *Top Income over the Twentieth Century: A Contrast Between European and English-Speaking Countries.* Oxford: Oxford University Press.

Atkinson, A. B., Piketty, T., & Saez, E. (2011). Top Incomes in the Long Run of History. *Journal of Economic Literature*, *49*(1), 3-71.

Barro, R. J. (1974). Are Government Bonds Net Wealth? *Journal of Political Economy*, *82*(6), 1095-1117.

Becker, G. S., & Tomes, N. (1979). An Equilibrium Theory of the Distribution of Income and Intergenerational Mobility. *Journal of Political Economy*, *87*(6), 1153-1189.

Becker, G. S., & Tomes, N. (1986). Human Capital and the Rise and Fall of Families. *Journal of Labor Economics*, *4*(3), S1-S39.

Behrman, J., & Taubman, P. (1985). Intergenerational Earnings Mobility in the United States: Some Estimates and a Test of Becker's Intergenerational Endowments Model. *The Review of Economics and Statistics*, *67*(1), 144-151.

Benabou, R. (2000). Unequal Societies: Income Distribution and the Social Contract. *American Economic Review*, *90*(1), 96-129.

Benabou, R., & Ok, E. A. (2001). Social Mobility and the Demand for Redistribution: The Poum Hypothesis. *Quarterly Journal of Economics, 116*(2), 447-487.

Benabou, R., & Tirole, J. (2006). Belief in a Just World and Redistributive Politics. *Quarterly Journal of Economics, 121*(2), 699-746.

Björklund, A., & Jäntti, M. (2000). Intergenerational mobility of socio-economic status in comparative perspective. *Nordic Journal of Political Economy, 26*, 3-32.

Björklund, A., Roine, J., & Waldenström, D. (2012). Intergenerational top income mobility in Sweden: Capitalist dynasties in the land of equal opportunities? *Journal of Public Economics, 96*(5-6), 474-484.

Black, S. E., & Devereux, P. J. (2010). Recent Developments in Intergenerational Mobility. In O. Ashenfelter & D. Card (Eds.), *Handbook of Labor Economics* (Vol. 4B). New York: North-Holland.

Blanden, J. (2005). International Evidence in Intergenerational Mobility. In *Essays on Intergenerational Mobility and its Variation across Time, Place and Family Structure.* London: University of London, PhD thesis.

Blanden, J. (2009). Intergenerational Income Mobility in a Comparative Perspective. In P. Dolton, R. Asplund, & E. Barth (Eds.), *Education and Inequality across Europe.* Cheltenham, UK: Edward Elgar Publishing Limited.

Blanden, J. (2013). Cross-Country Rankings in Intergenerational Mobility: A Comparison of Approaches from Economics and Sociology. *Journal of Economic Survey, 27*(1), 38-73.

Blanden, J., Gregg, P., & Macmillan, L. (2007). Accounting for Intergenerational Income Persistence: Noncognitive Skills, Ability and Education. *The Economic Journal, 117*(519), C43-C60.

Blanden, J., Haveman, R., Smeeding, T., & Wilson, K. (2014). Intergenerational Mobility in the United States and Great Britain: A Comparative Study of Parent-Child Pathways. *Review of Income and Wealth, 60*(3), 425-608.

Bowles, S., & Gintis, H. (2002). The Inheritance of Inequality. *Journal of Economic Perspectives, 16*(3), 3-30.

Bratsberg, B., Roed, K., Raaum, O., Naylor, R., Jäntti, M., Eriksson, T., & Österbacka, E. (2007). Nonlinearities in Intergenerational Earnings Mobility: Consequences for Cross-Country Comparisons. *Economic Journal, 117*(519), C72-C92.

CESifo. (2014). *Internationale Standardklassifikation des Bildungswesens (ISCED).* http://www.ifo.de/de/w/4SZvxCpgH. Accessed: June 6, 2014.

Checci, D., Ichino, A., & Rustichini, A. (1999). More equal but less mobile? Education financing and intergenerational mobility in Italy and in the US. *Journal of Public Economics, 74*(3), 351-393.

Corak, M. (2006). *Do Poor Children Become Poor Adults? Lessons from a Cross Country Comparison of Generational Earnings Mobility.* (IZA Discussion Paper No. 1993, Institute for the Study of Labor, University of Bonn)

Corneo, G. (2001). Inequality and the State: Comparing U.S. and German Preferences. *Annales d'Économie et de Statistique, 63-64*, 283-296.

Corneo, G. (2004). Wieso Umverteilung? Einsichten aus ökonometrischen Umfrageanalysen. In J. u. B. G. Brunner (Ed.), *Finanzpolitik und Umverteilung; Schriften des Vereins für Socialpolitik, Gesellschaft für Wirtschafts- und Sozialwissenschaften* (Vol. Band N.F. 301, p. 55-88). Duncker & Humblot, Berlin.

Corneo, G., & Grüner, H. P. (2002). Individual preferences for political redistribution. *Journal of Public Economics, 83*(1), 83-107.

Couch, K. A., & Dunn, T. A. (1997). Intergenerational Correlations in Labor Market Status: A Comparison of the United States and Germany. *The Journal of Human Resources, 32*(1), 210-232.

Fong, C. M. (2001). Social preferences, self-interest, and the demand for redistribution. *Journal of Public Economics, 82*(2), 225-246.

Fong, C. M. (2006). *Prospective Mobility, Fairness, and the Demand for Redistribution.* (Working Paper, Carnegie Mellon University, Pittsburgh)

Greene, W. H. (2000). *Econometric analysis.* Prentice Hall.

Guillaud, E. (2013). Preferences for redistribution: an empirical analysis over 33 countries. *Journal of Economic Inequality, 11*(1), 57-78.

Hertz, T., Jayasundera, T., Piraino, P., Selcuk, S., Smith, N., & Verashchagina, A. (2007). The Inheritance of Educational Inequality: International Comparisons and Fifty-Year Trends. *The B.E. Journal of Economic Analysis & Policy, 7*(2), Article 10.

Hirschman, A. O., & Rothschild, M. (1973). The Changing Tolerance for Income Inequality in the Course of Economic Development. *Quarterly Journal of Economics*, *87*(4), 544-566.

Hirvonen, L. (2010). *Accounting for Intergenerational Earnings Persistence: Can We Distinguish between Education, Skills, and Health?* (SOFI Working Paper 2/2010, Swedish Institute for Social Research, Stockholm University)

Kuhn, A. (2013). Inequality Perceptions, Distributional Norms, and Redistributive Preferences in East and West Germany. *German Economic Review*, *14*(4), 483-499.

Mayer, S. E., & Lopoo, L. M. (2008). Government spending and intergenerational mobility. *Journal of Public Economics*, *92*(1-2), 139-158.

Mazumder, B. (2005). Fortunate Sons: New Estimates of Intergenerational Mobility in the U.S. using Social Security Earnings Data. *Review of Economics and Statistics*, *87*(2), 235-255.

Meltzer, A. H., & Richard, S. F. (1981). A Rational Theory of the Size of Government. *Journal of Political Economy*, *89*(5), 914-927.

Pfarr, C. (2012). *Meltzer-Richard and social mobility hypothesis: revisting the income-redistribution nexus using German choice data.* (Discussion Paper 10-12, Universität Bayreuth, Rechts- und Wirtschaftswissenschaftliche Fakultät, Wirtschaftswissenschaftliche Diskussionpapiere)

Pfarr, C., Schmid, A., & Ulrich, V. (2013). *You can't always get what you want – East and West Germans' attitudes and preferences regarding the welfare state.* (Discussion Paper 03-13, Universität Bayreuth, Rechts- und Wirtschaftswissenschaftliche Fakultät, Wirtschaftswissenschaftliche Diskussionpapiere)

Piketty, T. (1995). Social Mobility and Redistributive Politics. *Quarterly Journal of Economics*, *110*(3), 551-584.

Piketty, T. (2014). *Capital in the Twenty-First Century.* Harvard University Press.

Rainer, H., & Siedler, T. (2008). Subjective income and employment expectations and preferences for redistribution. *Economic Letters*, *99*(3), 449-453.

Roberts, K. W. S. (1977). Voting Over Income Tax Schedules. *Journal of Public Economics*, *8*(3), 329-340.

Romer, T. (1975). Individual Welfare, Majority Voting, and the Properties of a Linear Income Tax. *Journal of Public Economics*, *4*(2), 163-185.

Schnitzlein, D. D. (2008). *Verbunden über Generationen: Struktur und Ausmaß der intergenerationellen Einkommensmobilität in Deutschland.* (SOEP-papers 80, DIW Berlin)

Solon, G. (1992). Intergenerational Income Mobility in the United States. *American Economic Review*, *82*(3), 393-408.

Solon, G. (1999). Intergenerational Mobility in the Labor Market. In O. Ashenfelter & D. Card (Eds.), *Handbook of Labor Economics* (Vol. 3A). Amsterdam: North-Holland.

Solon, G. (2002). Cross-Country Differences in Intergenerational Earnings Mobility. *Journal of Economic Perspectives*, *16*(3), 59-66.

Solon, G. (2004). A model of intergenerational mobility variation over time and place. In M. Corak (Ed.), *Generational Income Mobility in North America and Europe* (p. 38-47). Cambridge: Cambridge University Press.

Tabellini, G. (2008). The Scope of Cooperation: Values and Incentives. *Quarterly Journal of Economics*, *123*(3), 905-950.

Vogel, T. (2006). *Reassessing Intergenerational Mobility in Germany and the United States: the Impacts of Differences in Lifecycle Earnings Patterns* [Working Paper]. (SFB 649 Discussion Paper 2006-055, Freie Universität Berlin)

Weizsäcker, R. K. v. (1999). Chancengleichheit, Statusmobilität und öffentliche Bildungsinvestitionen. In D. Timmermann (Ed.), *Berufliche Weiterbildung in Europäischer Perspektive; Schriften des Vereins für Socialpolitik, Gesellschaft für Wirtschafts- und Sozialwissenschaften* (Vol. N.F. Band 267, p. 265-311). Duncker & Humblot, Berlin.

Wiegand, J. (1997). *Intergenerational earnings mobility in Germany.* (Mimeo, University College London, London)

Zimmerman, D. J. (1992). Regression Toward Mediocrity in Economic Stature. *American Economic Review*, *82*(3), 409-429.

Appendix

A Derivation of the Intergenerational Income Immobility

A.1 Income Elasticity in Absence of Public Education

Without governmental activity, incomes are related across generations as follows:

$$\log Y_{it} = y^* + \omega\phi \log Y_{it-1} + \varphi\, G_{it} \tag{A.1}$$

with:

$$y^* = \omega\phi \log(\frac{\gamma\omega\phi}{1+\gamma\omega\phi}), \tag{A.2}$$

$$G_{it} = g\, G_{it-1} + u_{it}^G. \tag{A.3}$$

According to theory, the intergenerational income elasticity η is derived by:[1]

$$\eta = \text{plim } b = \frac{Cov(\log Y_{it}, \log Y_{it-1})}{Var(\log Y_{it-1})}.$$

Considering Equation (A.1), it follows that:

$$\begin{aligned}
\eta &= \frac{Cov(y^* + \omega\phi\ \log Y_{it-1} + \varphi\, G_{it}, logY_{it-1})}{Var(\log Y_{it-1})} \\
&= \frac{\omega\phi\, Var(\log Y_{it-1}) + \varphi\, Cov(G_{it}, \log Y_{it-1})}{Var(\log Y_{it-1})} \\
&= \omega\phi + \varphi \cdot \frac{Cov(G_{it}, \log Y_{it-1})}{Var(\log Y_{it-1})}.
\end{aligned}$$

Considering Equation (A.3), $Cov(G_{it}, \log Y_{it-1})$ is described by:

$$\begin{aligned}
Cov(G_{it}, \log Y_{it-1}) &= Cov(gG_{it-1} + u_{it}^G, \log Y_{it-1}) \\
&= g\, Cov(G_{it-1}, \log Y_{it-1}) = g\, Cov(G_{it}, \log Y_{it}).
\end{aligned}$$

[1] See, for example, Greene (2000).

Taking account of (A.1), this turns into:

$$\begin{aligned} & Cov(G_{it}, \log Y_{it-1}) = g\, Cov(G_{it}, y^* + \omega\phi \log Y_{it-1} + \varphi\, G_{it}) \\ \Leftrightarrow \quad & Cov(G_{it}, \log Y_{it-1}) = g \cdot (\omega\phi\, Cov(G_{it}, \log Y_{it-1}) + \varphi\, Var(G_{it})) \\ \Rightarrow \quad & Cov(G_{it}, \log Y_{it-1}) = \frac{\varphi g}{1 - g\omega\phi} \cdot Var(G_{it}) = \frac{\varphi g}{1 - g\omega\phi} \cdot \frac{\sigma^2_{u^G}}{1 - g^2}. \end{aligned}$$

As in the long run $Var(logY_{it}) = Var(logY_{it-1})$, considering Equation (A.1), $Var(logY_{it})$ turns into:

$$Var(\log Y_{it}) = \omega^2\phi^2 Var(\log Y_{it-1}) + \varphi^2 Var(G_{it}) + 2\varphi\omega\phi Cov(G_{it}, \log Y_{it-1})$$

$$\begin{aligned} \Leftrightarrow (1 - \omega^2\phi^2)\, Var(\log Y_{it-1}) &= \varphi^2\, Var(G_{it}) + 2\varphi\omega\phi\, Cov(G_{it}, \log Y_{it-1}) \\ &= \varphi^2 \cdot \frac{\sigma^2_{u^G}}{1 - g^2} + 2\varphi\omega\phi \cdot \frac{\varphi g}{1 - g\omega\phi} \cdot \frac{\sigma^2_{u^G}}{1 - g^2} \\ &= \varphi^2 \cdot \frac{\sigma^2_{u^G}}{1 - g^2} \cdot (1 + \frac{2\omega\phi g}{1 - \omega\phi g}) \\ \Rightarrow \quad Var(logY_{it-1}) &= \frac{\sigma^2_{u^G}}{1 - g^2} \cdot \frac{\varphi^2(1 + \omega\phi g)}{(1 - \omega\phi g)(1 - \omega^2\phi^2)}. \end{aligned}$$

As a consequence, the intergenerational income elasticity η is:

$$\eta = \frac{\omega\phi + \varphi}{1 + \omega\phi\varphi}.$$

A.2 Public Education and Income Correlation across Generations

Crowding-Out of Public and Private Human Capital Investments

Assuming a crowding-out of public and private human capital investment, while taking into account the optimal level of private human capital investment, individual income of generation t is given by:

$$\begin{aligned}\log Y_{it} &= \omega\phi \cdot [\log(\frac{\gamma\omega\phi}{1+\gamma\omega\phi}) + \log((1-\tau)Y_{it-1} + B_{it}) + \varphi\, G_{it}] \\ &= \omega\phi \cdot [\log(\frac{\gamma\omega\phi}{1+\gamma\omega\phi}) + \log((1-\tau)Y_{it-1}(1 + \frac{B_{it}}{(1-\tau)Y_{it-1}}))] + \varphi\, G_{it}.\end{aligned}$$

For a sufficiently small $\frac{B_{it}}{(1-\tau)Y_{it-1}}$, this turns into:

$$\log Y_{it} \approx \omega\phi \cdot [\log(\frac{\gamma\omega\phi}{1+\gamma\omega\phi}) + \log((1-\tau)Y_{it-1}) + \frac{B_{it}}{(1-\tau)Y_{it-1}}] + \varphi\, G_{it}.$$

With $\frac{B_{it}}{(1-\tau)Y_{it-1}} \cong N - \nu \log Y_{it-1}$ finally $\log Y_{it}$ can be described by:

$$\begin{aligned}\log Y_{it} &\cong y_{co} + \omega\phi(1-\nu)\log Y_{it-1} + \varphi G_{it} \\ \text{with} \quad y_{co} &= \omega\phi(N + \log(\frac{\gamma\omega\phi}{1+\gamma\omega\phi} \cdot (1-\tau)).\end{aligned}$$

No Effect of Public Education on Private Human Capital Investment

Assuming that there is no effect of public education on private human capital investment, while taking into account the optimal level of private human capital investment, individual income of generation t is given by:

$$\begin{aligned}\log Y_{it} &= \omega\phi \log(\frac{\gamma\omega\phi}{1+\gamma\omega\phi}) + \omega\phi\log((1-\tau) \cdot Y_{it-1} \cdot B_{it}) + \varphi\, G_{it} \\ &= \omega\phi \log(\frac{\gamma\omega\phi}{1+\gamma\omega\phi}) + \omega\phi\log((1-\tau)^2 \cdot Y_{it-1}^2 \cdot \frac{B_{it}}{(1-\tau)Y_{it-1}}) + \varphi\, G_{it}.\end{aligned}$$

With $\frac{B_{it}}{(1-\tau)y_{it-1}} \cong N - \nu \log Y_{it-1}$, this turns into:

$$\begin{aligned}\log Y_{it} &= \omega\phi \log(\frac{\gamma\omega\phi}{1+\gamma\omega\phi}) + \varphi\, G_{it} \\ &\quad + \omega\phi(2\log((1-\tau)Y_{it-1}) + \log(N - \nu \log Y_{it-1}) \\ &= \omega\phi \log(\frac{\gamma\omega\phi}{1+\gamma\omega\phi}) + \varphi\, G_{it} \\ &\quad + \omega\phi(2\log((1-\tau)Y_{it-1}) + \log N + \log(1 - \frac{\nu}{N}\log Y_{it-1}))\end{aligned}$$

For $\frac{\nu}{N}$ to be sufficiently small it follows that:

$$\begin{aligned}\log Y_{it} &= \omega\phi \log(\frac{\gamma\omega\phi}{1+\gamma\omega\phi}) + \varphi\, G_{it} \\ &\quad + \omega\phi(2\log((1-\tau)Y_{it-1}) + \log N + \frac{\nu}{N}\log Y_{it-1}))\end{aligned}$$

and thus,

$$\begin{aligned}&\log Y_{it} \cong y_{nr} + \omega\phi(2 - \frac{\nu}{N})\log Y_{it-1} + \varphi G_{it} \\ &\text{with} \quad y_{nr} = \omega\phi \log(2(1-\tau)\cdot N \cdot \frac{\gamma\omega\phi}{1+\gamma\omega\phi}).\end{aligned}$$

B Sequential Decomposition of Income Immobility

Table B.1: German Women - Descriptive Statistics

Average parental income at 10 and 16	34,797
(standard deviation)	(13,827)
Average sons' earnings at 30 and 34	18,410
(standard deviation)	(12,532)
At least high school graduate	85.3%
At least some college	39.9%
Graduate college/ Degree	29.4%
Education missing	4.3%
Married at age 22 or less	11.0%
Missing married at 22	2.0%
Ages 22-25 No labor/ education	20.5%
Ages 22-25 Full-time work/ education	67.1%
Ages 26-29 No labor/ education	21.9%
Ages 26-29 Full-time work/ education	61.5%
Missing labor market info	0.2%
Married at 30	48.5%
Missing married at 30	2.0%
Health excellent at 30	14.5%
Health poor plus fair at 30	6.2%
Health missing at 30	2.4%
Higher managerial and professional at 30	11.4%
Lower managerial and professional or higher at 30	39.4%
Intermediate occupation or higher at 30	66.4%
Small employers and self-employed or higher at 30	68.9%
Lower supervisory and technical occupation or higher at 30	70.6%
Semi-routine occupation or higher at 30	92.2%
Missing occupation at 30	30.8%
Higher managerial and professional at 34	7.7%
Lower managerial and professional or higher at 34	29.0%
Intermediate occupation or higher at 34	45.7%
Small employers and self-employed or higher at 34	49.0%
Lower supervisory and technical occupation or higher at 34	49.5%
Semi-routine occupation or higher at 34	63.1%
Missing occupation at 34	23.4%

Notes: Monetary values for Germany are given in year 2000 euros. Means of the variables are only the means of the observations not missing. As appropriate, missing values are replaced with these mean values in the empirical analysis.

Table B.2: German Women - Income Persistence

Elasticity (β)	Correlation (ρ)
0.286** (0.117)	0.102** (0.010)

Significance levels: *** < 0.01, ** < 0.05, and * < 0.1.

Table B.3: German Women - Education Decomposition

Factors	Effect of parental income on factor (λ)	Return to factor (γ)	Percent of total β
*Ed*1: "at least high school"	0.152*** (0.030)	0.213 (0.138)	11.3%
*Ed*2: "at least some college"	0.460*** (0.052)	0.234 (0.148)	37.7%
*Ed*3: "completed college"	0.379*** (0.050)	0.076 (0.153)	10.0%
Education total			59.0%

Significance levels: *** < 0.01, ** < 0.05, and * < 0.1.

Table B.4: German Women - Sequential Decomposition

Explained components of total β	(1) Part of total β	(1) Percent of total β	(2) Part of total β	(2) Percent of total β	(3) Part of total β	(3) Percent of total β	(4) Part of total β	(4) Percent of total β
Education	0.169**	59.0%	0.147**	51.5%	0.081	28.3%	0.081	28.4%
	(0.070)	(7.9)	(0.068)	(7.0)	(0.535)	(11.1)	(0.055)	(15.8)
Early marriage			0.018	6.3%	−0.040	−13.8%	−0.040	−13.9%
			(0.035)	(1.0)	(0.028)	(3.1)	(0.026)	(6.1)
Labour market attachment, ages 22-25			0.059	20.5%	0.023	8.2%	0.026	9.0%
			(0.059)	(2.0)	(0.033)	(3.5)	(0.036)	(3.3)
Labour market attachment, ages 26-29					0.075	26.3%	0.078	27.2%
					(0.082)	(2.7)	(0.089)	(1.0)
Marriage and health at 30					0.009	3.3%	0.007	2.3%
					(0.037)	(1.5)	(0.036)	(12.6)
Occupation at age 30					0.021	7.3%	0.012	4.1%
					(0.054)	(7.4)	(0.061)	(8.4)
Occupation at age 34							0.043	15.0%
							(0.035)	(4.8)
Missing values	−0.020	−6.9%	−0.020	−6.9%	0.043	14.9%	0.058	20.2%
	(0.031)	(0.6)	(0.034)	(1.9)	(0.050)	(1.5)	(0.054)	(17.4)
Explained component of β	0.169**	59.0%	0.224***	78.3%	0.170	59.6%	0.206	72.1%
	(0.070)	(7.9)	(0.079)	(8.8)	(0.117)	(18.9)	(0.123)	(28.8)
Unexplained component of β	0.137	47.9%	0.082**	28.6%*	0.073	25.5%	0.022	7.7%
	(0.180)	(7.7)	(0.168)	(7.6)	(0.121)	(0.2)	(0.120)	(32.2)
Total β	0.286***		0.286***		0.286***		0.286***	

Significance levels: *** < 0.01, ** < 0.05, and * < 0.1.

Table B.5: German Men - Sequential Decomposition Using Family Income

	(1)		(2)		(3)		(4)	
Explained components of total β	Part of total β	Percent of total β	Part of total β	Percent of total β	Part of total β	Percent of total β	Part of total β	Percent of total β
Education	0.067**	21.7%	0.086***	27.6%	0.082***	26.5%	0.074**	23.9%
	(0.029)	(0.3)	(0.030)	(1.1)	(0.030)	(0.4)	(0.029)	(1.2)
Early marriage			−0.007	−2.3%	−0.005	−1.7%	−0.005	−1.7%
			(0.008)	(0.2)	(0.006)	(0.1)	(0.006)	(2.9)
Labour market attachment, ages 22-25			0.008	2.6%	0.000	0.1%	−0.001	−0.4%
			(0.027)	(0.3)	(0.017)	(0.1)	(0.017)	(0.1)
Labour market attachment, ages 26-29					0.019	6.2%	0.020	6.5%
					(0.026)	(0.1)	(0.028)	(65.3)
Marriage and health at 30					−0.011	−3.6%	−0.012	−3.8%
					(0.014)	(0.1)	(0.015)	(4.4)
Occupation at age 30					0.044	14.3%	0.032	10.4%
					(0.039)	(0.3)	(0.039)	(15.8)
Occupation at age 34							−0.001	−0.3%
							(0.025)	(55.6)
Missing values	−0.004	−1.2%	−0.005	−1.5%	0.010	3.4%	0.011	3.5%
	(0.014)	(0.6)	(0.010)	(0.1)	(0.024)	(0.2)	(0.025)	(45.2)
Explained component of β	0.067**	21.7%***	0.087**	27.9%	0.130**	41.7%	0.107*	34.6%
	(0.029)	(0.3)	(0.040)	(0.7)	(0.060)	(0.5)	(0.063)	(253.6)
Unexplained component of β	0.247**	79.5%	0.229**	73.6%*	0.170	54.9%	0.192*	61.9%
	(0.108)	(0.5[illegible]	(0.110)	(0.720)	(0.105)	(0.388)	(0.099)	(298.7)
Total β	0.311***		0.311***		0.311***		0.311***	

Significance levels: *** < 0.01, ** < 0.05, and * < 0.1.

Table B.6: German Men - Education Decomposition Results Using Years in School or Training

Factors	Effect of parental income on factor (λ)	Return to factor (γ)	Percent of total β
"at least 9 years"	0.003 (0.013)	0.612*** (0.195)	0.6%
"at least 10 years"	0.085*** (0.030)	0.152 (0.107)	4.7%
"at least 11 years"	0.137*** (0.038)	0.069 (0.090)	3.4%
"at least 13 years"	0.252*** (0.041)	−0.397*** (0.090)	−36.3%
"at least 15 years"	0.219*** (0.037)	0.453*** (0.117)	35.9%
"at least 17 years"	0.268*** (0.031)	0.140 (0.115)	13.6%
Education total			21.9%

Significance levels: *** < 0.01, ** < 0.05, and * < 0.1.

Table B.7: German Men - Education Decomposition Results Using Educational Attainment, Secondary Stage

Factors	Effect of parental income on factor (λ)	Return to factor (γ)	Percent of total β
at least "Haupt-schulabschluss"	0.004 (0.013)	0.646*** (0.191)	1.0%
at least "Real-schulabschluss"	0.106*** (0.038)	0.160** (0.077)	6.1%
at least "Fach-hochschulreife"	0.215*** (0.041)	−0.202* (0.114)	−15.7%
at least "Allgemeine Hochschulreife"	0.262*** (0.039)	0.222* (0.114)	21.1%
Education total			12.5%

Significance levels: *** < 0.01, ** < 0.05, and * < 0.1.

Table B.8: German Men - Earnings by Occupational Level (Age 30)

Higher managerial and professional	35,963 (35,963)
Lower managerial and professional or higher	34,842 (33,674)
Intermediate occupation or higher	34,168 (31,290)
Small employers and self-employed or higher	34,386 (36,051)
Lower supervisory and technical occupation or higher	33,981 (30,109)
Semi-routine occupation or higher	32,048 (28,046)
Routine occupation	27,053 (27,053)
Missing occupation	17,356 (17,356)

Notes: Monetary values for Germany are given in year 2000 euros. Means of the variables are only the means of the observations not missing. As appropriate, missing values are replaced with these mean values in the empirical analysis.

Table B.9: German Men - Occupation Decomposition Results Using European ESeC Categorization

Factors	Effect of parental income on factor (λ)	Return to factor (γ)	Percent of total β
*Occ*1 (lowest level)	0.141*** (0.029)	0.051 (0.094)	3.5%
*Occ*2	0.190*** (0.038)	0.068 (0.137)	5.1%
*Occ*3	0.206*** (0.039)	−0.183 (0.170)	−13.7%
*Occ*4	0.200*** (0.040)	−0.011 (0.164)	−0.8%
*Occ*5	0.147*** (0.041)	0.138 (0.143)	7.4%
*Occ*6	0.145*** (0.040)	−0.084 (0.106)	−4.4%
*Occ*7 (highest level)	0.238*** (0.033)	0.238*** (0.090)	20.5%

Significance levels: *** < 0.01, ** < 0.05, and * < 0.1.

Table B.10: International Comparison - Descriptive Statistics for Main Variables (Men)

	Germany	Great Britain	United States
Average parental income	34,939	391.62	72,017
(standard deviation)	(16,060)	(190.73)	(48,723)
Average sons' earnings	28,956	475.96	44,527
(standard deviation)	(16,931)	(314.57)	(38,642)
At least high school graduate	81.9%	74.1%	88.7%
At least some college	38.0%	43.7%	53.0%
Graduate college/ Degree	29.9%	23.4%	29.1%
Education missing	6.6%	6.4%	1.4%
Married at age 22 or less	5.2%	5.4%	31.3%
Missing married at 22	2.6%	5.2%	17.3%
No labor/ education at 22-25	17.6%	5.8%	22.9%
Full-time work/ education at 22-25	67.8%	88.1%	64.5%
No labor/ education at 26-29	12.7%	2.8%	7.5%
Full-time work/ education at 26-29	74.9%	71.5%	84.5%
Missing labor market info	0.3%	6.2%	2.3%
Married at 30	34.7%	38.3%	66.7%
Missing married at 30	6.2 %	7.6%	2.0%
Health excellent at 30	15.7%	33.2%	34.2%
Health poor plus fair at 30	4.8%	13.0%	4.2%
Health missing at 30	6.2%	6.2%	3.8%
*Occ*6 (highest level) at 30	19.0%	15.4%	16.3%
*Occ*5 at 30	37.4%	45.7%	40.0%
*Occ*4 at 30	46.1%	55.6%	49.0%
*Occ*3 at 30	52.1%	56.6%	58.9%
*Occ*2 at 30	57.6%	77.7%	71.7%
*Occ*1 (lowest level) at 30	85.4%	88.2%	85.9%
Missing occupation at 30	16.7%	9.2%	12.5%
*Occ*6 (highest level) at 34	17.0%	22.4%	17.7%
*Occ*5 at 34	31.9%	51.9%	41.0%
*Occ*4 at 34	37.9%	59.3%	51.2%
*Occ*3 at 34	42.8%	63.1%	60.3%
*Occ*2 at 34	46.9%	81.1%	73.9%
*Occ*1 (lowest level) at 34	65.3%	90.4%	88.3%
Missing occupation at 34	10.2%	19.5%	5.4%

Notes: Monetary amounts for Germany are given in year 2000 euros, for Great Britain in year 2000 pounds, and for the United States in year 2000 dollars. For Great Britain, income/earnings are quoted weekly (hence comparison is obtained by multiplying the results by 52). Means of the variables are only the means of the observations not missing. As appropriate, missing values are replaced with these mean values in the empirical analysis.

Table B.11: Great Britain - Sequential Decomposition

	(1)		(2)		(3)		(4)	
Explained components of total β	Part of total β	Percent of total β	Part of total β	Percent of total β	Part of total β	Percent of total β	Part of total β	Percent of total β
Education	0.086	29.3%	0.090	30.5%	0.050	17.0%	0.034	11.6%
	(0.006)	(2.4)	(0.007)	(2.5)	(0.005)	(1.9)	(0.005)	(1.7)
Early marriage			−0.001	−0.4%	−0.001	−0.2%	−0.001	−0.2%
			(0.001)	(0.3)	(0.001)	(0.3)	(0.001)	(0.3)
Labour market attachment, ages 22-25			0.011	3.7%	0.006	2.1%	0.007	2.3%
			(0.004)	(1.3)	(0.002)	(0.8)	(0.003)	(0.9)
Labour market attachment, ages 26-29					0.009	3.1%	0.008	2.9%
					(0.003)	(1.0)	(0.003)	(1.0)
Marriage and health at 30					0.004	1.2%	0.003	1.1%
					(0.002)	(0.6)	(0.002)	(0.6)
Occupation at age 30					0.065	21.9%	0.044	15.0%
					(0.005)	(2.0)	(0.005)	(1.7)
Occupation at age 34							0.057	19.3%
							(0.005)	(1.9)
Missing values	0.001	0.4%	0.002	0.8%	0.002	0.7%	0.002	0.8%
	(0.001)	(0.4)	(0.002)	(0.5)	(0.001)	(0.5)	(0.001)	(0.5)
Explained component of β	0.086	29.3%	0.100	33.8%	0.133	45.2%	0.153	51.8%
	(0.006)	(2.4)	(0.007)	(2.6)	(0.009)	(2.9)	(0.010)	(3.1)
Unexplained component of β	0.207	70.3%	0.193	65.3%	0.159	54.1%	0.140	47.4%
	(0.017)	(2.3)	(0.017)	(2.6)	(0.015)	(2.9)	(0.015)	(3.1)
Total β	0.295		0.295		0.295		0.295	

Significance levels: *** < 0.01, ** < 0.05, and * < 0.1.
Results presented in this table are taken from Blanden et al. (2014).

Table B.12: United States - Sequential Decomposition

Explained components of total β	(1) Part of total β	(1) Percent of total β	(2) Part of total β	(2) Percent of total β	(3) Part of total β	(3) Percent of total β	(4) Part of total β	(4) Percent of total β
Education	0.185 (0.027)	48.1% (8.7)	0.191 (0.029)	49.6% (9.2)	0.116 (0.029)	30.1% (8.1)	0.101 (0.030)	26.3% (8.5)
Early marriage			0.006 (0.013)	1.6% (3.4)	0.006 (0.011)	1.5% (3.0)	0.007 (0.011)	1.8% (2.9)
Labour market attachment, ages 22-25			−0.007 (0.009)	−1.9% (2.4)	−0.011 (0.008)	−2.8% (2.2)	−0.011 (0.008)	−2.7% (2.2)
Labour market attachment, ages 26-29					0.017 (0.014)	4.5% (3.5)	0.016 (0.014)	4.2% (3.4)
Marriage and health at 30					0.003 (0.008)	0.9% (2.1)	0.005 (0.008)	1.2% (2.0)
Occupation at age 30					0.073 (0.020)	18.9% (5.3)	0.052 (0.019)	13.5% (5.0)
Occupation at age 34							0.040 (0.022)	10.3% (5.8)
Missing values	0.000 (0.003)	0.1% (0.8)	−0.003 (0.008)	−0.8% (2.1)	0.012 (0.014)	3.1% (3.6)	0.016 (0.150)	4.1% (3.9)
Explained component of β	0.185 (0.027)	48.1% (8.7)	0.190 (0.266)	49.3% (8.8)	0.204 (0.036)	52.9% (8.9)	0.210 (0.039)	54.6% (9.5)
Unexplained component of β	0.199 (0.056)	51.8% (8.8)	0.198 (0.057)	51.5% (9.0)	0.169 (0.052)	44.0% (9.6)	0.159 (0.051)	41.3% (10.3)
Total β	0.385		0.385		0.385		0.385	

Significance levels: $^{***} < 0.01$, $^{**} < 0.05$, and $^{*} < 0.1$.
Results presented in this table are taken from Blanden et al. (2014).

C Beliefs Regarding Income Determinants

C.1 Derivation of the Expected Utility

For agents born into low-income families, expected utility EU_{it} is:

$$EU_{it}\Big|_{y_{it-1}=y_L} = (1-\tau_t)Ey_{it}\Big|_{y_{it-1}=y_L} + \tau_t Y_t - C(e_{it}) + \gamma E y_{it+1}$$

with

$$Ey_{it}\Big|_{y_{it-1}=y_L} = \rho_{Lt}\cdot\Delta y + y_L$$

and

$$Ey_{it+1} = \rho_{Lt}\cdot(\rho_{Ht+1}\cdot\Delta y + y_L) + (1-\rho_{Lt})\cdot(\rho_{Lt+1}\cdot\Delta y + y_L).$$

Taking into account the probabilities of success dependent on social origins, $\rho_{L\cdot}$ and $\rho_{H\cdot}$, as given by Equations (8.1) and (8.2), the expected utility of agents born into low income families can be described by:

$$\begin{aligned} EU_{it}\Big|_{y_{it-1}=y_L} &= (1-\tau_t)((\pi_L+\theta e_{Lt})\Delta y + y_L) + \tau_t Y_t - \frac{1}{2a}e_{Lt}^2 \\ &\quad + \gamma((\pi_L+\theta e_{Lt})(\rho_{Ht+1}-\rho_{Lt+1})\Delta y + \rho_{Lt+1}\Delta y + y_L). \quad \text{(C.1)} \end{aligned}$$

Analogously, for agents born into high-income families, expected utility is given by:

$$EU_{it}\Big|_{y_{it-1}=y_H} = (1-\tau_t)Ey_{it}\Big|_{y_{it-1}=y_H} + \tau_t Y_t - C(e_{it}) + \gamma E y_{it+1}$$

with

$$Ey_{it}\Big|_{y_{it-1}=y_H} = \rho_{Ht}\cdot\Delta y + y_L$$

and

$$Ey_{it+1} = \rho_{Ht}\cdot(\rho_{Ht+1}\cdot\Delta y + (1-\rho_{Ht+1})y_L) + (1-\rho_{Ht})\cdot(\rho_{Lt+1}\cdot\Delta y + y_L).$$

Taking into account the probabilities of success dependent on social origins, $\rho_{L\cdot}$ and $\rho_{H\cdot}$, as given by Equations (8.1) and (8.2) yields the following expected utility of agents born into high income families:

$$\begin{aligned} EU_{it}\Big|_{y_{it-1}=y_H} &= (1-\tau_t)((\pi_L+\Delta\pi+\theta e_{Ht})\Delta y+y_L)+\tau_t Y_t-\frac{1}{2a}e_{Ht}^2 \\ &+\gamma((\pi_L+\Delta\pi+\theta e_{Ht})(\rho_{Ht+1}-\rho_{Lt+1})\Delta y+\rho_{Lt+1}\Delta y+y_L). \qquad (C.2) \end{aligned}$$

C.2 Derivation of the Social Welfare Function

When voting over the tax rate for the next generation τ_t, the social welfare function given by Equation (8.5) is:

$$\begin{aligned} V_t &= (1-\delta)((1-\tau_t)Ey_{it}\Big|_{y_{it-1}=y_L}+\tau_t EY_t-C(e_t)+\gamma E[y_{t+1}]) \\ &+\delta((1-\tau_t)Ey_{it}\Big|_{y_{it-1}=y_H}+\tau_t EY_t-C(e_t)+\gamma E[y_{it+1}]) \qquad (C.3) \end{aligned}$$

Taken into account the expected utilities for both groups of agents, as derived in Equations (C.1) and (C.2), as well as the expected average income EY_t with:

$$EY_t = y_L+(\pi_L+\theta e_t)\Delta y+H_t\Delta\pi\Delta y,$$

and the optimal effort level:

$$e_t = (1-\tau_t)\theta a\Delta y+\gamma\Delta\pi\theta a\Delta y,$$

the social welfare function in Equation (C.3) turns into:

$$\begin{aligned} V_t &= y_L(1+\gamma)+\pi_L\Delta y(1+\gamma(1+\Delta\pi))+\tau H_t\Delta\pi\Delta y+\gamma\theta e_{t+1}\Delta y \\ &+(1-\tau_t+\gamma\Delta\pi)\cdot[\frac{1}{2}a\theta^2\Delta y^2(1+\tau_t+\gamma\Delta\pi)+\delta\Delta y\Delta\pi] \end{aligned}$$

C.3 Inequality of Opportunity and Incentives to Work

If the determinants of personal economic success are known in society, the optimal level of individual effort is:

$$e = (1 - \tau_t)\theta a \Delta y + \gamma \Delta \pi a \theta \Delta y.$$

In this case, the chosen tax rate is:

$$\tau_t = \frac{(H_t - \delta)\Delta \pi}{a\theta^2 \Delta y}.$$

The effect of reducing inequality of opportunity on the individual effort level is given by:

$$\frac{\partial e}{\partial \Delta \pi} = -\frac{H_t - \delta}{\theta} + \gamma a \theta \Delta y < 0 \quad \Leftrightarrow \quad (H_t - \delta) > \gamma \theta^2 a \Delta y.$$

Considering that $H_t - \delta \leq \frac{\Delta y \theta^2 a}{\Delta \pi}$ (as resulting from $\tau_t \leq 1$), $\frac{\partial e}{\partial \Delta \pi} < 0$, if:

$$\gamma < \frac{1}{\Delta \pi},$$

which is always fulfilled, as $0 < \gamma, \Delta \pi < 1$.

C.4 Long-Term Equilibrium and its Influencing Factors

At first, changes in individual effort, the tax rate, and the income distribution within a society yield indirect effects for each other factor. The impact of changes in individual effort is as follows:

$$e_{i\infty} \uparrow \;\Rightarrow\; \overline{e}_{\infty} \uparrow \;\Rightarrow\; H_{\infty} \uparrow \;\Rightarrow\; \tau_{\infty} \uparrow.$$

The impact of changes in the tax rate is as follows:

$$\tau_{\infty} \uparrow \;\Rightarrow\; e_{i\infty} \downarrow \;\Rightarrow\; H_{\infty} \downarrow.$$

The impact of changes in the income distribution is as follows:

$$H_{\infty} \uparrow \;\Rightarrow\; \tau_{\infty} \uparrow \;\Rightarrow\; e_{i\infty} \downarrow.$$

In the long run, the tax rate, the effort level of dynasty i, and the share of high-income class members of society are:

$$\tau_\infty = \frac{(\theta^*(1+\gamma\Delta\pi^*)\overline{\theta}_\infty a\Delta y + \pi_L^* - \delta(1-\Delta\pi^*))\Delta\pi^*}{(\overline{\theta}_\infty(\overline{\theta}_\infty(1-\Delta\pi^*)+\theta^*\Delta\pi^*))a\Delta y\overline{\theta}_\infty},$$

$$e_{i\infty} = \theta(\mu_{i\infty})\frac{(1-\Delta\pi^*)\cdot(a\Delta y\overline{\theta}_\infty^2(1+\gamma\Delta\pi^*)+\delta\Delta\pi^*)-\pi_L^*\Delta\pi^*}{\overline{\theta}_\infty(\overline{\theta}_\infty(1-\Delta\pi^*)+\theta^*\Delta\pi^*)},$$

$$H_\infty = \frac{\pi_L^*\overline{\theta}_\infty + \theta^*\overline{\theta}_\infty^2 a\Delta y(1+\gamma\Delta\pi^*)+\delta\theta^*\Delta\pi^*}{\overline{\theta}_\infty(1-\Delta\pi^*)+\theta^*\Delta\pi^*}.$$

Changes in the cost parameter a yield the following aggregate effects:

$$\frac{\partial e_\infty}{\partial a} = \theta(\mu_{i\infty})\cdot\frac{(1-\Delta\pi^*)\Delta y\overline{\theta}_\infty(1+\gamma\Delta\pi^*)}{\overline{\theta}_\infty(1-\Delta\pi^*)+\theta^*\Delta\pi^*} > 0,$$

$$\frac{\partial H_\infty}{\partial a} = \frac{\theta^*\overline{\theta}_\infty^2\Delta y(1+\gamma\Delta\pi^*)}{\overline{\theta}_\infty(1-\Delta\pi^*)+\theta^*\Delta\pi^*} > 0, \quad \text{and}$$

$$\frac{\partial \tau_\infty}{\partial a} = -\frac{(\pi_L^*-\delta(1-\Delta\pi^*))\Delta\pi^*}{(\overline{\theta}_\infty(1-\Delta\pi^*)+\theta^*\Delta\pi^*)a^2\Delta y\overline{\theta}_\infty} < 0.$$

Note that $\frac{\partial \tau_\infty}{\partial a} < 0$ is always fulfilled, as $\pi_L^* > \delta(1-\Delta\pi^*)$ results from the assumption of a nonnegative tax rate (that is, $\tau > 0$).

Changes in the income disparity Δy yield the following aggregate effects:

$$\frac{\partial e_\infty}{\partial \Delta y} = \theta(\mu_{i\infty})\cdot\frac{(1-\Delta\pi^*)a\overline{\theta}_\infty(1+\gamma\Delta\pi^*)}{\overline{\theta}_\infty(1-\Delta\pi^*)+\theta^*\Delta\pi^*} > 0, \quad \text{and}$$

$$\frac{\partial H_\infty}{\partial \Delta y} = \frac{\theta^*\overline{\theta}_\infty^2 a(1+\gamma\Delta\pi^*)}{\overline{\theta}_\infty(1-\Delta\pi^*)+\theta^*\Delta\pi^*} > 0,$$

$$\frac{\partial \tau_\infty}{\partial \Delta y} = -\frac{(\pi_L^*-\delta(1-\Delta\pi^*))\Delta\pi^*}{(\overline{\theta}_\infty(1-\Delta\pi^*)+\theta^*\Delta\pi^*)a\Delta y^2\overline{\theta}_\infty} < 0.$$

Note that $\frac{\partial \tau_\infty}{\partial \Delta y} < 0$ is always fulfilled, as $\pi_L^* > \delta(1-\Delta\pi^*)$ results from the assumption of a nonnegative tax rate ($\tau > 0$).

Assuming $a = \Delta y = 1$, respective τ_∞, $e_{i\infty}$, and H_∞ turns into:

$$\tau_\infty = \frac{(\theta^*(1+\gamma\Delta\pi^*)\overline{\theta}_\infty + \pi_L^* - \delta(1-\Delta\pi^*))\Delta\pi^*}{(\overline{\theta}_\infty(\overline{\theta}_\infty(1-\Delta\pi^*) + \theta^*\Delta\pi^*))\overline{\theta}_\infty},$$

$$e_{i\infty} = \theta(\mu_{i\infty})\frac{(1-\Delta\pi^*)\cdot(\overline{\theta}^2_\infty(1+\gamma\Delta\pi^*) + \delta\Delta\pi^*) - \pi_L^*\Delta\pi^*}{\overline{\theta}_\infty(\overline{\theta}_\infty(1-\Delta\pi^*) + \theta^*\Delta\pi^*)},$$

$$H_\infty = \frac{\pi_L^*\overline{\theta}_\infty + \theta^*\overline{\theta}^2_\infty(1+\gamma\Delta\pi^*) + \delta\theta^*\Delta\pi^*}{\overline{\theta}_\infty(1-\Delta\pi^*) + \theta^*\Delta\pi^*}.$$

Effect of Dynastic Altruism

$$\frac{\partial\tau_\infty}{\partial\gamma} = \frac{\theta^*\Delta\pi^{*2}}{\overline{\theta}_\infty(1-\Delta\pi^*) + \theta^*\Delta\pi^*} > 0$$

$$\frac{\partial e_{i\infty}}{\partial\gamma} = \theta(\mu_{i\infty})\cdot\frac{(1-\Delta\pi^*)\Delta\pi^*\overline{\theta}_\infty}{\overline{\theta}_\infty(1-\Delta\pi^*) + \theta^*\Delta\pi^*} > 0$$

$$\frac{\partial H_\infty}{\partial\gamma} = \frac{\theta^*\overline{\theta}^2_\infty\Delta\pi^*}{\overline{\theta}_\infty(1-\Delta\pi^*) + \theta^*\Delta\pi^*} > 0$$

Effect of Varying Social Value Judgment

$$\frac{\partial\tau_\infty}{\partial\delta} = -\frac{(1-\Delta\pi^*)\Delta\pi^*}{(\overline{\theta}_\infty(1-\Delta\pi^*) + \theta^*\Delta\pi^*)\overline{\theta}_\infty} < 0$$

$$\frac{\partial e_{i\infty}}{\partial\delta} = \theta(\mu_{i\infty})\cdot\frac{(1-\Delta\pi^*)\Delta\pi^*}{(\overline{\theta}_\infty(1-\Delta\pi^*) + \theta^*\Delta\pi^*)\overline{\theta}_\infty} > 0$$

$$\frac{\partial H_\infty}{\partial\delta} = \frac{\theta^*\Delta\pi^*}{\overline{\theta}_\infty(1-\Delta\pi^*) + \theta^*\Delta\pi^*} > 0$$

Effect of the Basic Predetermined Factor

$$\frac{\partial \tau_\infty}{\partial \pi_L^*} = \frac{\Delta\pi^*}{(\overline{\theta}_\infty(1-\Delta\pi^*)+\theta^*\Delta\pi^*)\overline{\theta}_\infty} > 0$$
$$\frac{\partial e_{i\infty}}{\partial \pi_L^*} = -\theta(\mu_{i\infty})\frac{(1-\Delta\pi^*)\Delta\pi^*}{(\overline{\theta}_\infty(1-\Delta\pi^*)+\theta^*\Delta\pi^*)\overline{\theta}_\infty} < 0$$
$$\frac{\partial H_\infty}{\partial \pi_L^*} = \frac{\overline{\theta}_\infty}{\overline{\theta}_\infty(1-\Delta\pi^*)+\theta^*\Delta\pi^*} > 0$$

Effect of the Real Role of Effort

$$\frac{\partial \tau_\infty}{\partial \theta^*} = \frac{\Delta\pi^*(\overline{\theta}^2_\infty(1-\Delta\pi^*)(1+\gamma\Delta\pi^*)+\delta\Delta\pi^*(1-\Delta\pi^*)-\pi_L^*\Delta\pi^*)}{(\overline{\theta}_\infty(1-\Delta\pi^*)+\theta^*\Delta\pi^*)^2\overline{\theta}_\infty}$$
$$\frac{\partial e_{i\infty}}{\partial \theta^*} = -\theta(\mu_{i\infty})\frac{((1-\Delta\pi^*)(\overline{\theta}^2_\infty(1+\gamma\Delta\pi^*)+\delta\Delta\pi^*)-\pi_L^*\Delta\pi^*)\Delta\pi^*}{(\overline{\theta}_\infty(1-\Delta\pi^*)+\theta^*\Delta\pi^*)^2\overline{\theta}_\infty}$$
$$\frac{\partial H_\infty}{\partial \theta^*} = \frac{\overline{\theta}_\infty(\overline{\theta}_\infty(1-\Delta\pi^*)(1+\gamma\Delta\pi^*)+\delta\Delta\pi^*)}{(\overline{\theta}_\infty(1-\Delta\pi^*)+\theta^*\Delta\pi^*)^2}$$

It follows that $\frac{\partial \tau_\infty}{\partial \theta^*} > 0$, $\frac{\partial e_{i\infty}}{\partial \theta^*} < 0$, and $\frac{\partial H_\infty}{\partial \theta^*} > 0$ if:

$$\pi_L^* < \delta(1-\Delta\pi^*) + (1+\gamma\Delta\pi^*)\overline{\theta}^2_\infty\frac{1-\Delta\pi^*}{\Delta\pi^*},$$

which is always fulfilled because of the assumption $\tau \leq 1$.

Effect of the Socially Believed Role of Effort

$$\frac{\partial \tau_\infty}{\partial \overline{\theta}_\infty} = -\frac{\Delta\pi^*\theta^*(1-\Delta\pi^*)\cdot(1+\gamma\Delta\pi^*)\cdot(2\overline{\theta}_\infty(1-\Delta\pi^*)+\theta^*\Delta\pi^*)}{(\overline{\theta}_\infty(1-\Delta\pi^*)+\theta^*\Delta\pi^*)^2} - \frac{(\pi_L^*-\delta(1-\Delta\pi^*))\cdot(2\overline{\theta}_\infty(1-\Delta\pi^*)+\theta^*\Delta\pi^*)}{\overline{\theta}_\infty^2(\overline{\theta}_\infty(1-\Delta\pi^*)+\theta^*\Delta\pi^*)^2}$$

$$\frac{\partial e_{i\infty}}{\partial \overline{\theta}_\infty} = \theta(\mu_{i\infty})\cdot[\frac{\Delta\pi^*\theta^*(1-\Delta\pi^*)\cdot(1+\gamma\Delta\pi^*)\cdot(2\overline{\theta}_\infty(1-\Delta\pi^*)+\theta^*\Delta\pi^*)}{(\overline{\theta}_\infty(1-\Delta\pi^*)+\theta^*\Delta\pi^*)^2} + \frac{(\pi_L^*-\delta(1-\Delta\pi^*))\cdot(2\overline{\theta}_\infty(1-\Delta\pi^*)+\theta^*\Delta\pi^*)}{\overline{\theta}_\infty^2(\overline{\theta}_\infty(1-\Delta\pi^*)+\theta^*\Delta\pi^*)^2}]$$

$$\frac{\partial H_\infty}{\partial \overline{\theta}_\infty} = \frac{\theta^*(\overline{\theta}_\infty^2(1-\Delta\pi^*)+2\theta^*\overline{\theta}_\infty\Delta\pi^*)(1+\gamma\Delta\pi^*)}{(\overline{\theta}_\infty(1-\Delta\pi^*)+\theta^*\Delta\pi^*)^2} + \frac{\theta^*(\pi_L^*-\delta(1-\Delta\pi^*))\Delta\pi^*}{(\overline{\theta}_\infty(1-\Delta\pi^*)+\theta^*\Delta\pi^*)^2}$$

It follows that $\frac{\partial \tau_\infty}{\partial \overline{\theta}_\infty} < 0$ and $\frac{\partial e_{i\infty}}{\partial \overline{\theta}_\infty} > 0$ if:

$$\delta < \delta^* = \frac{\pi_L^*}{1-\Delta\pi^*} + \frac{\theta^*\overline{\theta}_\infty^2(1+\gamma\Delta\pi^*)}{2\overline{\theta}_\infty(1-\Delta\pi^*)\theta^*\Delta\pi^*}$$

Thus, only if δ is above the critical value δ^*, the tax rate will decrease and effort will increase with an increasing $\overline{\theta}_\infty$. Moreover, it follows that $\frac{\partial H_\infty}{\partial \overline{\theta}_\infty} > 0$ if:

$$\delta < \frac{\pi_L^*}{1-\Delta\pi^*} + \frac{2\theta^*\overline{\theta}_\infty(1+\gamma\Delta\pi^*)}{1-\Delta\pi^*} + \frac{\overline{\theta}_\infty^2(1+\gamma\Delta\pi^*)}{\Delta\pi^*},$$

which is always fulfilled because of the assumption $\tau > 0$.

Effect of Inequality of Opportunity

$$\frac{\partial \tau_\infty}{\partial \Delta\pi^*} = \frac{\theta^*(\overline{\theta}_\infty(1+\gamma\Delta\pi^*(2-\Delta\pi^*))+\theta^*\gamma\Delta\pi^*)}{(\overline{\theta}_\infty(1-\Delta\pi^*)+\theta^*\Delta\pi^*)^2} - \frac{\delta(\overline{\theta}_\infty(1-\Delta\pi^*)^2+\theta^*\Delta\pi^{*2})+\pi_L^*\overline{\theta}_\infty}{\overline{\theta}_\infty(\overline{\theta}_\infty(1-\Delta\pi^*)+\theta^*\Delta\pi^*)^2}$$

$$\frac{\partial e_{i\infty}}{\partial \Delta\pi^*} = \theta(\mu_{i\infty})\cdot\frac{(\pi_L^*+\theta^*\overline{\theta}_\infty)\overline{\theta}_\infty-(\delta+\gamma\overline{\theta}_\infty)\cdot(\overline{\theta}_\infty(1-\Delta\pi^*)^2+\theta^*\Delta\pi^{*2})}{\overline{\theta}_\infty(\overline{\theta}_\infty(1-\Delta\pi^*)+\theta^*\Delta\pi^*)^2}$$

$$\frac{\partial H_\infty}{\partial \Delta\pi^*} = \frac{\overline{\theta}_\infty(\theta^*\overline{\theta}_\infty^2\gamma+(\pi_L^*+\theta^*\overline{\theta}_\infty)(\overline{\theta}_\infty-\theta^*)+\delta\theta^*)}{(\overline{\theta}_\infty(1-\Delta\pi^*)+\theta^*\Delta\pi^*)^2}$$

First, $\frac{\partial \tau_\infty}{\partial \Delta\pi^*} > 0$ is obviously fulfilled for $\overline{\theta}_\infty < \theta^*(\frac{\Delta\pi^*}{1-\Delta\pi^*})^2$. The same holds true for $\overline{\theta}_\infty > \theta^*(\frac{\Delta\pi^*}{1-\Delta\pi^*})^2$ if:

$$\delta < \frac{\overline{\theta}_\infty(\pi_L^*+\theta^*)(\overline{\theta}_\infty(1+\gamma\Delta\pi^*(2-\Delta\pi^*))+\theta^*\gamma\Delta\pi^*)}{\overline{\theta}_\infty(1-\Delta\pi^*)^2+\theta^*\Delta\pi^{*2}},$$

which is always fulfilled due to the assumption $\tau > 0$.
Second, $\frac{\partial e_{i\infty}}{\partial \Delta\pi^*} < 0$ is always fulfilled for $\overline{\theta}_\infty < \theta^*(\frac{\Delta\pi^*}{1-\Delta\pi^*})^2$. The same holds true for $\overline{\theta}_\infty > \theta^*(\frac{\Delta\pi^*}{1-\Delta\pi^*})^2$ only if:

$$\delta\frac{1}{\overline{\theta}_\infty}+\gamma\overline{\theta}_\infty < \frac{\pi_L^*+\theta^*\overline{\theta}_\infty}{\overline{\theta}_\infty(1-\Delta\pi^*)^2+\theta^*\Delta\pi^{*2}}.$$

Third, $\frac{\partial H_\infty}{\partial \Delta\pi^*} > 0$ is always fulfilled for $\overline{\theta}_\infty > \theta^*$. The same holds true for $\overline{\theta}_\infty < \theta^*$ only if

$$(\delta+\gamma\overline{\theta}_\infty^2)\theta^* > (\pi_L^*+\theta^*\overline{\theta}_\infty)(\theta^*-\overline{\theta}_\infty).$$

Probability of Upward Mobility

The probability of upward mobility is defined by:

$$\begin{aligned}\overline{\rho}_L^* &= \pi_L^* + \theta^* \cdot \overline{e}(\overline{\theta}_\infty) \\ &= \pi_L^* + \theta^* \frac{(1-\Delta\pi^*)[\overline{\theta}_\infty^2(1+\gamma\Delta\pi^*) + \delta\Delta\pi^*] - \pi_L^*\Delta\pi^*}{\overline{\theta}_\infty(1-\Delta\pi^*) + \theta^*\Delta\pi^*}.\end{aligned}$$

The effects of γ, δ, and π_L^* on $\overline{\rho}_L^*$ are given by:

$$\begin{aligned}\frac{\partial\overline{\rho}_L^*}{\partial\gamma} &= \frac{\theta^*\overline{\theta}_\infty^2(1-\Delta\pi^*)\Delta\pi^*}{\overline{\theta}_\infty(1-\Delta\pi^*) + \theta^*\Delta\pi^*} > 0, \\ \frac{\partial\overline{\rho}_L^*}{\partial\delta} &= \frac{\theta^*(1-\Delta\pi^*)\Delta\pi^*}{\overline{\theta}_\infty(1-\Delta\pi^*) + \theta^*\Delta\pi^*} > 0, \\ \frac{\partial\overline{\rho}_L^*}{\partial\pi_L^*} &= 1 - \frac{\theta^*\Delta\pi^*}{\overline{\theta}_\infty(1-\Delta\pi^*) + \theta^*\Delta\pi^*} > 0.\end{aligned}$$

Changes in θ^* and $\overline{\theta}_\infty$ affect $\overline{\rho}_L^*$ as follows:

$$\frac{\partial\overline{\rho}_L}{\partial\theta^*} = \frac{((\overline{\theta}_\infty^2(1+\gamma\Delta\pi^*) + \delta\Delta\pi^*)(1-\Delta\pi^*) - \pi_L^*\Delta\pi_L^*)\overline{\theta}_\infty(1-\Delta\pi^*)}{(\overline{\theta}_\infty(1-\Delta\pi^*) + \theta^*\Delta\pi^*)^2} > 0,$$

which is always fulfilled, as $\pi_L^* < \delta(1-\Delta\pi^*) + \frac{1-\Delta\pi^*}{\Delta\pi^*}\overline{\theta}_\infty^2(1+\gamma\Delta\pi^*)$ holds true resulting from the assumption $\tau \leq 1$.

$$\begin{aligned}\frac{\partial\overline{\rho}_L}{\partial\overline{\theta}_\infty} = &\frac{\theta^*(1-\Delta\pi^*)((\overline{\theta}_\infty^2(1-\Delta\pi^*) + 2\theta^*\overline{\theta}_\infty\Delta\pi^*)(1+\gamma\Delta\pi^*))}{(\overline{\theta}_\infty(1-\Delta\pi^*) + \theta^*\Delta\pi^*)^2} \\ &+ \frac{\theta^*(1-\Delta\pi^*)(\pi_L^*\Delta\pi^* - \delta\Delta\pi^*(1-\Delta\pi^*))}{(\overline{\theta}_\infty(1-\Delta\pi^*) + \theta^*\Delta\pi^*)^2} > 0,\end{aligned}$$

which is always fulfilled, as $\delta < \frac{\pi_L^*}{1-\Delta\pi^*} + \frac{\overline{\theta}_\infty^2(1+\gamma\Delta\pi^*)}{\Delta\pi^*} + 2\frac{\theta^*\overline{\theta}_\infty(1+\gamma\Delta\pi^*)}{1-\Delta\pi^*}$ holds true resulting from the assumption $\tau > 0$.
Finally, changes in $\Delta\pi^*$ affects $\overline{\rho}_L^*$ as follows:

$$\frac{\partial\overline{\rho}_L}{\partial\Delta\pi^*} = -\frac{\theta^*((\pi_L^* + \theta^*\overline{\theta}_\infty)\overline{\theta}_\infty - (\gamma\overline{\theta}_\infty^2 + \delta)\cdot(\theta^*\Delta\pi^{*2}) - \overline{\theta}_\infty(1-\Delta\pi^*)^2)}{(\overline{\theta}_\infty(1-\Delta\pi^*) + \theta^*\Delta\pi^*)^2}$$

Thus, $\frac{\partial \overline{\rho}_L}{\partial \Delta\pi^*} < 0$ if

$$\pi_L^* + \theta^*\overline{\theta}_\infty > (\gamma\overline{\theta}_\infty + \delta\frac{1}{\overline{\theta}_\infty})(\theta^*\Delta\pi^{*2} - \overline{\theta}_\infty(1-\Delta\pi^*)^2)$$

which is always fulfilled for $\overline{\theta}_\infty \leq \theta^*(\frac{\Delta\pi^*}{1-\Delta\pi^*})^2$. The same holds true for $\overline{\theta}_\infty > \theta^*(\frac{\Delta\pi^*}{1-\Delta\pi^*})^2$ if:

$$\gamma < \frac{\overline{\theta}_\infty(\pi_L^* + \theta^*\overline{\theta}_\infty) + \delta\theta^*\Delta\pi^*}{\overline{\theta}_\infty^2(\overline{\theta}_\infty(1-\Delta\pi^*)^2 - \theta^*\Delta\pi^{*2})}.$$

Probability of Downward Mobility

The probability of downward mobility is defined by:

$$(1-\overline{\rho}_H^*) = 1 - \Delta\pi^* - \overline{\rho}_L^*$$

with

$$\overline{\rho}_L^* = (\pi_L^* + \theta^*\frac{(1-\Delta\pi^*)[\overline{\theta}_\infty^2(1+\gamma\Delta\pi^*) + \delta\Delta\pi^*] - \pi_L^*\Delta\pi^*}{\overline{\theta}_\infty(1-\Delta\pi^*) + \theta^*\Delta\pi^*}).$$

The effects of γ, δ, and π_L^* on $(1-\overline{\rho}_H^*)$ are given by:

$$\frac{\partial(1-\overline{\rho}_H)}{\partial\gamma} = -\frac{\theta^*\overline{\theta}_\infty^2(1-\Delta\pi^*)\Delta\pi^*}{\overline{\theta}_\infty(1-\Delta\pi^*) + \theta^*\Delta\pi^*} < 0$$

$$\frac{\partial(1-\overline{\rho}_H)}{\partial\delta} = -\frac{\theta^*(1-\Delta\pi^*)\Delta\pi^*}{\overline{\theta}_\infty(1-\Delta\pi^*) + \theta^*\Delta\pi^*} < 0$$

$$\frac{\partial(1-\overline{\rho}_H)}{\partial\pi_L^*} = -(1 - \frac{\theta^*\Delta\pi^*}{\overline{\theta}_\infty(1-\Delta\pi^*) + \theta^*\Delta\pi^*}) < 0$$

Changes in θ^* and $\overline{\theta}_\infty$ affect $(1-\overline{\rho}_H^*)$ as follows:

$$\frac{\partial(1-\overline{\rho}_H)}{\partial\theta^*} = -\frac{((\overline{\theta}_\infty^2(1+\gamma\Delta\pi^*) + \delta\Delta\pi^*)(1-\Delta\pi^*) - \pi_L^*\Delta\pi_L^*)\overline{\theta}_\infty(1-\Delta\pi^*)}{(\theta^*\Delta\pi^* - \overline{\theta}_\infty(1-\Delta\pi^*))^2}.$$

$\frac{\partial(1-\overline{\rho}_H)}{\partial\theta^*} < 0$ is always fulfilled, as $\pi_L^* < \delta(1-\Delta\pi^*) + \frac{1-\Delta\pi^*}{\Delta\pi^*}\overline{\theta}_\infty^2(1+\gamma\Delta\pi^*)$ holds true resulting from the assumption $\tau \leq 1$.

$$\frac{\partial(1-\overline{\rho}_H)}{\partial\overline{\theta}_\infty} = -\frac{\theta^*(1-\Delta\pi^*)\cdot(\overline{\theta}_\infty(\overline{\theta}_\infty(1-\Delta\pi^*)+2\theta^*\Delta\pi^*)\cdot(1+\gamma\Delta\pi^*))}{(\overline{\theta}_\infty(1-\Delta\pi^*)+\theta^*\Delta\pi^*)^2} - \frac{\theta^*(1-\Delta\pi^*)\cdot(\pi_L^*\Delta\pi^* - \delta\Delta\pi^*(1-\Delta\pi^*))}{(\overline{\theta}_\infty(1-\Delta\pi^*)+\theta^*\Delta\pi^*)^2} < 0$$

which is always fulfilled, as $\delta < \frac{\pi_L^*}{1-\Delta\pi^*} + \frac{\overline{\theta}_\infty^2(1+\gamma\Delta\pi^*)}{\Delta\pi^*} + 2\frac{\theta^*\overline{\theta}_\infty(1+\gamma\Delta\pi^*)}{1-\Delta\pi^*}$ holds true resulting from the assumption $\tau > 0$.
Finally, changes in $\Delta\pi^*$ affects $(1-\overline{\rho}_H^*)$ as follows:

$$\frac{\partial(1-\overline{\rho}_H)}{\partial\Delta\pi^*} = \frac{(\pi_L^*+\theta^*\overline{\theta}_\infty)\theta^*\overline{\theta}_\infty - (\overline{\theta}_\infty(1-\Delta\pi^*)+\theta^*\Delta\pi^*)^2}{(\overline{\theta}_\infty(1-\Delta\pi^*)+\theta^*\Delta\pi^*)^2} - \frac{(\gamma\overline{\theta}_\infty^2+\delta)\theta^*(\overline{\theta}_\infty(1-\Delta\pi^*)^2 - \theta^*\Delta\pi^{*2})}{(\overline{\theta}_\infty(1-\Delta\pi^*)+\theta^*\Delta\pi^*)^2}$$

Thus, $\frac{\partial(1-\overline{\rho}_H)}{\partial\Delta\pi^*} > 0$ hold true for $\overline{\theta}_\infty \left\{ \begin{matrix} < \\ > \end{matrix} \right\} \theta^*(\frac{\Delta\pi^*}{1-\Delta\pi^*})^2$ if

$$(\gamma\overline{\theta}_\infty + \delta\frac{1}{\overline{\theta}_\infty})\left\{ \begin{matrix} > \\ < \end{matrix} \right\} \frac{\theta^*\overline{\theta}_\infty(\pi_L^*+\theta^*\overline{\theta}_\infty) - (\overline{\theta}_\infty(1-\Delta\pi^*)+\theta^*\Delta\pi^*)^2}{\theta^*\overline{\theta}_\infty(\overline{\theta}_\infty(1-\Delta\pi^*)^2 - \theta^*\Delta\pi^{*2})},$$

Mobility

The mobile part of society is given by:

$$M = (\pi_L^* + \theta^*\cdot\frac{(1-\Delta\pi^*)(\overline{\theta}_\infty^2(1+\gamma\Delta\pi^*)+\delta\Delta\pi^*) - \pi_L^*}{\overline{\theta}_\infty(1-\Delta\pi^*)+\theta^*\Delta\pi^*}) \cdot (1 - \frac{\pi_L^*\overline{\theta}_\infty + \theta^*(\overline{\theta}_\infty^2(1+\gamma\Delta\pi^*)+\delta\Delta\pi^*)}{\overline{\theta}_\infty(1-\Delta\pi^*)+\theta^*\Delta\pi^*})$$

The effects of γ, δ, and π_L^* on M are given by:

$$\frac{\partial M}{\partial \gamma} = \frac{2\pi_L^*\theta^*\overline{\theta}_\infty^2\Delta\pi^*(\overline{\theta}_\infty(1-\Delta\pi^*)+\theta^*\overline{\theta}_\infty^2(1+\gamma\Delta\pi^*)(1-\Delta\pi^*))}{(\theta^*\Delta\pi^*+\overline{\theta}_\infty(1-\Delta\pi^*))^2} + \frac{2(\theta^*\Delta\pi^*(1-\Delta\pi^*)\delta)\theta^*\overline{\theta}_\infty^2\Delta\pi^*}{(\theta^*\Delta\pi^*+\overline{\theta}_\infty(1-\Delta\pi^*))^2} > 0,$$

$$\frac{\partial M}{\partial \delta} = \frac{2\theta^*\Delta\pi^*(\pi_L^*\overline{\theta}_\infty(1-\Delta\pi^*)-\theta^*\overline{\theta}_\infty^2(1+\gamma\Delta\pi^*)(1-\Delta\pi^*))}{(\theta^*\Delta\pi^*+\overline{\theta}_\infty(1-\Delta\pi^*))^2} - \frac{2(\theta^*\Delta\pi^*(1-\Delta\pi^*)\delta)\theta^*\Delta\pi^*}{(\theta^*\Delta\pi^*+\overline{\theta}_\infty(1-\Delta\pi^*))^2} > 0,$$

$$\frac{\partial M}{\partial \pi_L^*} = \frac{2\overline{\theta}_\infty(\pi_L^*\overline{\theta}_\infty(1-\Delta\pi^*)+\theta^*\overline{\theta}_\infty^2(1+\gamma\Delta\pi^*)(1-\Delta\pi^*))}{(\overline{\theta}_\infty(1-\Delta\pi^*)+\theta^*\Delta\pi^*)^2} + \frac{2(\theta^*\Delta\pi^*(1-\Delta\pi^*)\delta)\overline{\theta}_\infty}{(\overline{\theta}_\infty(1-\Delta\pi^*)+\theta^*\Delta\pi^*)^2} > 0.$$

Assuming $\gamma = \delta = 0$, changes in θ^* and $\overline{\theta}_\infty$ affect M as follows:

$$\frac{\partial M}{\partial \theta^*} = \frac{2\overline{\theta}_\infty^2(\pi_L^*(1-\Delta\pi^*)((\overline{\theta}_\infty(1-\Delta\pi^*)+\theta^*\Delta\pi^*)\overline{\theta}_\infty-\pi_L^*\Delta\pi^*))}{(\theta^*\Delta\pi^*+\overline{\theta}_\infty(1-\Delta\pi^*))^3} + \frac{2\overline{\theta}_\infty^2(\theta^*\overline{\theta}_\infty^3(1-\Delta\pi^*)^2)}{(\theta^*\Delta\pi^*+\overline{\theta}_\infty(1-\Delta\pi^*))^3} > 0,$$

which is always fulfilled due to the assumption that $\tau \leq 1$, and:

$$\frac{\partial M}{\partial \overline{\theta}} = \frac{2\theta^*\overline{\theta}_\infty(\pi_L^*(1-\Delta\pi^*)(\overline{\theta}_\infty(3\theta^*\Delta\pi^*+\overline{\theta}_\infty(1-\Delta\pi^*))+\pi_L^*\Delta\pi^*))}{(\theta^*\Delta\pi^*+\overline{\theta}_\infty(1-\Delta\pi^*))^3} + \frac{2\theta^*\overline{\theta}_\infty(\theta^*\overline{\theta}_\infty^2(1-\Delta\pi^*)(2\theta^*\Delta\pi^*+\overline{\theta}_\infty(1-\Delta\pi^*)))}{(\theta^*\Delta\pi^*+\overline{\theta}_\infty(1-\Delta\pi^*))^3} > 0.$$

Finally, changes in $\Delta\pi^*$ affects M as follows:

$$\frac{\partial M}{\partial \Delta\pi^*} = -\frac{\overline{\theta}_\infty^2(\pi_L^*+\theta^*\overline{\theta}_\infty)^2(\theta^*(2-\Delta\pi^*)-\overline{\theta}_\infty(1-\Delta\pi^*))}{(\theta^*\Delta\pi^*+\overline{\theta}_\infty(1-\Delta\pi^*))^3}$$

$$\frac{\partial M}{\partial \Delta\pi^*} < 0 \quad \text{if} \quad \theta^*(2-\Delta\pi^*) > \overline{\theta}_\infty(1-\Delta\pi^*)$$

Generally, with $\gamma > 0$ and $\delta > 0$ will $\frac{\partial M}{\partial \Delta\pi^*} < 0$ if:

$$\begin{aligned}&\overline{\theta}_\infty^2(\pi_L^* + \theta^*\overline{\theta}_\infty)^2(\overline{\theta}_\infty(1-\Delta\pi^*) - \theta^*(2-\Delta\pi^*)\\&+ 2\theta^*\overline{\theta}_\infty(\delta + \gamma\overline{\theta}_\infty^2)(\pi_L^* + \theta^*\overline{\theta}_\infty)(\overline{\theta}_\infty(1-\Delta\pi^*) - \theta^*\Delta\pi^*)\\&+ \theta^{*2}\Delta\pi^*(\delta + \gamma\overline{\theta}_\infty^2)^2(\overline{\theta}_\infty(2-\Delta\pi^*)(1-\Delta\pi^*) - \theta^*\Delta\pi^{*2}) < 0\end{aligned}$$

For $\gamma = 0$, $\delta = 0$, and $\pi_L^* > 0$ will $\frac{\partial M}{\partial \Delta\pi^*} < 0$ if:

$$\overline{\theta}_\infty < \theta^*\frac{2-\Delta\pi^*}{1-\Delta\pi^*}.$$

For $\gamma > 0$, $\delta = 0$, and $\pi_L^* = 0$ will $\frac{\partial M}{\partial \Delta\pi^*} < 0$ if:

$$\overline{\theta}_\infty < \theta^*\frac{2(1+\gamma\Delta\pi^*) - \Delta\pi^*(1-\gamma^2\Delta\pi^{*2})}{(1-\Delta\pi^*)(1+\gamma(2\gamma\Delta\pi^*(1-\Delta\pi^*)))}.$$

For $\gamma = 0$, $\delta > 0$, and $\pi_L^* = 0$ will $\frac{\partial M}{\partial \Delta\pi^*} < 0$ if:

$$\overline{\theta}_\infty < \theta^*\frac{\Delta\pi^*(2\overline{\theta}_\infty^2 + \delta\Delta\pi^*)}{(1-\Delta\pi^*)(2\overline{\theta}_\infty^2 + \delta\Delta\pi^*(2-\Delta\pi^*))}.$$

MIX
Papier aus verantwortungsvollen Quellen
Paper from responsible sources
FSC® C105338

If you have any concerns about our products,
you can contact us on
ProductSafety@springernature.com

In case Publisher is established outside the EU,
the EU authorized representative is:
Springer Nature Customer Service Center GmbH
Europaplatz 3, 69115 Heidelberg, Germany

Printed by Libri Plureos GmbH
in Hamburg, Germany